Charismatic and Expository Preaching

Charismatic and Expository Preaching
A Case Study of Two Preaching Methods within the Local Church

Lewis D. Mathis

WIPF & STOCK · Eugene, Oregon

CHARISMATIC AND EXPOSITORY PREACHING
A Case Study of Two Preaching Methods Within the Local Church

Copyright © 2022 Lewis D. Mathis. All rights reserved. Except for brief quotations in critical publications or reviews, no part of this book may be reproduced in any manner without prior written permission from the publisher. Write: Permissions, Wipf and Stock Publishers, 199 W. 8th Ave., Suite 3, Eugene, OR 97401.

Wipf & Stock
An Imprint of Wipf and Stock Publishers
199 W. 8th Ave., Suite 3
Eugene, OR 97401

www.wipfandstock.com

PAPERBACK ISBN: 978-1-6667-3611-3
HARDCOVER ISBN: 978-1-6667-9398-7
EBOOK ISBN: 978-1-6667-9399-4

Copyright for Fair Use Act

All Scripture quotations are taken from the Holy Bible, New International Version®, NIV®. Copyright ©1973, 1978, 1984, 2011 by Biblica, Inc.™ Used by permission of Zondervan. All rights reserved worldwide. www.zondervan.com. The "NIV" and "New International Version" are trademarks registered in the United States Patent and Trademark Office by Biblica, Inc.™

05/09/22

A special dedication to the late

Bishop Kenny McKnight

for putting my feet on the path
of the knowledge of Christ.

Contents

Preface | xi
Acknowledgments | xiii

Chapter 1: Introduction | 1
    Introduction   1
    Ministry Context   4
        Statement of the Problem   6
        Statement of Delimitations   9
        Statement of Limitations   10
    Theoretical Basis   10
        Statement of Methodology   13
        Review of Literature   14
        Scripture References   20

Chapter 2: Expository and Charismatic Preaching | 25
    Expository Preaching   27
        Expository Preaching Provides Authority and Power   30
        Expository Preaching Is Preaching a Revelatory Truth   31
    Charismatic Preaching   33
        Charismatic Movement   34
        Theological Issues with the Charismatic Movement   36
        Charismatics Biblical Interpretation Argument   39
        Glossolalia: "Speaking in Tongues"   44

CONTENTS

  Arguments against Charismatic Exegesis
  (Interpretation) 49
  The Holy Spirit Validates Both Preaching Methods 53
 Conclusion 56

Chapter 3: Issues That Divide Charismatic
  and Expository Preaching | 59
 Purpose and Objectives of the Research's Intervention 61
 People Involved: Purposive Sampling 62
 Biblical Task 64
 Combining Both Preaching Methods 76
 Conclusion 79

Chapter 4: Research Data Analysis | 84
 Purpose of This Study 84
 Review of Case-Study Research by Chapter 86
 Review of the Results from Interviews and Questionnaires 87
  Analysis of Interview Responses 88
  Analysis of Questionnaire Responses 102
 Final Analysis of Case-Study Findings 104
 Conclusion 106

Chapter 5: Final Conclusion and Findings | 107
 Introduction 107
 Finding 1 108
 Finding 2 109
 Results Compared to Previous Studies
 in This Literature Review 110
 Final Conclusion 116

CONTENTS

Appendix A: Research Interview Questions | 119
Appendix B: Research Questionnaire | 121
Appendix C: Consent Form (Pastor) | 123
Appendix D: Consent Form (Church Member) | 128
IRB Approval | 134
Vita | 136
Bibliography | 137

Preface

Preaching, by far, is the primary tool used within the body of Christ to spread the gospel throughout the world and draw people to the ecclesia (church). For centuries, the fundamental approach to heralding the word of God has been rooted in expository preaching. This theologically sound approach has been shadowed by the rise of the charismatic movement and its preaching. Therefore, the focus of this thesis-project study is indicated by the title: *Charismatic and Expository Preaching: A Case Study of Two Preaching Methods within the Local Church*. This study is necessary to determine if these two forms of preaching can coexist and if charismatic preaching can be incorporated as sound doctrinal preaching to edify the body of Christ.

The case study will be accomplished by theoretically and theologically comparing the data, conducting biblical research, and visiting charismatic and expository churches. This research aims to compare the two by evaluating the churches' growth and decline using these forms of preaching and how the congregants receive the preaching of the two. The results will be valuable to the ministry in understanding the effectiveness of the two as pertains to the church's growth and Christ as its foundation. New Hope Missionary Baptist Church was once considered charismatic and had tremendous growth, with its pastor being charismatic and possessing many of the spiritual gifts that congregants gravitated to with awe. With his departure, the church had a significant decline.

Acknowledgments

Thanks to my Lord and Savior, Jesus Christ, who provided the strength needed to get this far; without God, I could not have made it this far.

Thanks to my loving wife of twenty-five years, Phyllis Mathis, who has supported me throughout my academic journey. I dedicate this project to her for encouraging me to press on and complete the task—for always telling me that I could do it, to focus, and to do the work.

Thanks to my mentor, Dr. Jeffrey Cockrell, who has been with me throughout this endeavor.

Thanks to Pastor Walter Spencer with his words of wisdom and encouragement when I felt like giving up and when I felt unworthy, to Deacon Gary Sherman, and to my entire church family for their support and prayers.

Thanks to all the pastors, deacons, and church members who participated in this project, such as Pastor James Payne, Deacon Leroy Dawson, and the Zion Sisters Baptist Church members. Pastor Lorenzo Watson, Deacon W. D. Ford, and the members of Mount Olive Baptist Church. Thank you all for taking the time to help me with this project.

Thanks to my mother, Marzella Mathis; my brother, Ruffus Mathis; and my sister, Linda Mathis.

Chapter 1: Introduction

Introduction

Expository preaching has been the foundational tool for centuries within the church in conveying the word of God to its congregants. However, the emerging charismatic movement and its preaching have caused great concern regarding the fundamentals of the Bible's expository preaching. Considering this movement, charismatic preachers see tremendous growth in their ministries. In many local churches, pastors who hold steadfastly to expository preaching are experiencing a considerable decline in their churches.

Therefore, the need for this research is relevant to studying these methods of preaching to determine if they can coexist as a firm preaching method. Thus, charismatic preaching has great potential for being incorporated into some mode of expository preaching that is biblically sound and creates church growth. This study will help New Hope Missionary Baptist Church tremendously, considering that formerly, the church was charismatic under the church's previous pastor.

The research project aims to conduct a case study of two preaching methods by exploring the charismatic movement's humble beginnings originating from the Azusa Street Revival and by understanding the fundamentals of expository preaching. Today, "[the] Charismatic movement has been transformed into the fastest-growing segment of Christianity in America and throughout much of the world."[1] According to Mohler, "some

---

1. Mohler, "Charismatic Movement," para. 1.

experts estimate that the movement includes almost a half-billion adherents worldwide."[2] This movement has incorporated traditional Pentecostals, the Assemblies of God, and strong influences in Southern Baptist churches.[3] Although Mohler's article is dated in the year 2000, the statistics provided are relevant in showing how effective the charismatic movement was and how it has changed the church. However, concerning expository preaching, James F. Stitzinger has said, "Historical study of expository preaching begins with a proper understanding of the record of preaching in Scripture. Preaching in the Bible is in two basic forms: revelatory preaching and explanatory preaching."[4] These terms will be defined later within the contents of this research.

All postbiblical preaching has the backdrop of the preaching recorded in Scripture and must trace its roots to this source.[5] The Bible is the source of preaching; charismatics and expository preachers must draw from that source. That being the case, why is there a decline in local churches firmly rooted in expository preaching but an increase in charismatic churches? Therefore, the study is relevant in understanding why Christians are gravitating toward charismatic preaching and worship instead of expository-based preaching and worship. Visiting charismatic and expository-based churches, seeing how worship services flow, interviewing the pastors and chairpersons of the deacon board, getting questionnaires answered by congregants, and doing biblical research will be a starting point to answering this question.

Most local churches have pastors that are firm in expository preaching. They are preaching the word of God with clarity, and excellent hermeneutical skills are paramount in revealing the author's original intent to their congregants, not adding or taking away from the passage to fit their needs or justify their actions. Nonetheless, with this sound doctrine preached from an informative-based method, these churches experience no growth.

2. Mohler, "Charismatic Movement," para. 1.
3. Mohler, "Charismatic Movement," paras. 2–3.
4. Stitzinger, "History of Expository Preaching," 7.
5. Stitzinger, "History of Expository Preaching," 7.

CHAPTER 1: INTRODUCTION

Only the faithful few stay. Therefore, how could this be? When expository preaching illuminates the Scriptures, it clarifies God's word for those in attendance. Merrill F. Unger, being an advocate for expository preaching, asserts:

> Expository preaching gives the preacher authority and power. Holy Scripture as inspired by God, literally "God-breathed" (2 Tim 3:16), possesses a potent quality when preached by one who believes what he preaches is, in truth, the "Word of God." The authority and power which the inspired oracles possess become manifest in the pulpit ministry of the faithful Bible expositor. He speaks, yet the thrilling fact is true. God at the same time speaks through Him. He is conscious of inadequacy yet finds his task attended by divine authority. He is aware of the weakness but discovers the power of God operating in the Word he preaches, which is living and active, and sharper than any two-edged sword piercing even to the dividing of soul and Spirit, of both joints and marrow, quick to discern the thoughts and intents of the heart (Heb 4:12).[6]

Unger argues for results from their preaching. People, by the Holy Spirit's movement, should gravitate or be drawn to the message, becoming a part of that assembly/church and causing growth. However, the charismatic approach and its preaching acknowledges Scripture (God's word) as authoritative in concert with expository preaching. The charismatic asserts more emphasis on the Holy Spirit's movement, or baptism in the Spirit, by evidence of speaking in tongues (glossolalia) and the work it was sent to do (gifts of the Holy Spirit) in empowering Christ's church. Expository preachers hold to the centrality of *Sola scriptura* as foundational to sound preaching while not denying the Holy Spirit's works and the hermeneutics of charismatics concerning pneumatology and spiritual experience. Unger's article, although dated 1954, is essential in understanding the very foundation of expository preaching in this modern era.

---

6. Unger, "Expository Preaching," 324.

Charismatics' understanding of the Holy Spirit is the dividing factor between these two preaching methods. Charismatics believe the empowering of the Holy Spirit is a subsequent event in the conversion of the believer. In other words, Charismatics believe there is a baptism of the Spirit as a "second blessing" or experience that occurs after salvation.[7] They also think that a believer must possess spiritual gifts, such as healing with the laying on of hands and especially speaking in tongues, as evidence of their conversion into the body of Christ.

Although there is a significant concern from a hermeneutical perspective concerning this argument, one cannot overlook the charismatic doctrine's effectiveness, which has generated tremendous growth in the church. The charismatic movement cannot be ignored from a biblical perspective because of its foundational recognition of Scripture being authoritative; thus, the fact that it stands on God's word, with spiritual charisma provided by the Holy Spirit, institutes merit for this method of preaching. Therefore, it is the purpose of this research to find common ground between these two preaching methods and determine if they can coexist as one sound doctrine from a biblical perspective for the growth and empowerment of Christ's church.

Ministry Context

This research will benefit New Hope Missionary Baptist Church (NHMBC) and other small local churches. However, being a member of New Hope for nineteen years, I have observed tremendous growth and decline of the church throughout the years. The former pastor, who without a doubt was tremendously charismatic in his preaching style, influenced many people to know Christ and to join the church. With his angelic voice when singing, his Spirit-filled preaching, and his invoking of the Holy Spirit in all aspects of the worship service, one could feel and witness God's mighty presence and the Holy Spirit throughout the sanctuary.

---

7. Mohler, "Charismatic Movement," para. 2.

CHAPTER 1: INTRODUCTION

This pastor's approach was twofold: he approached God's word first in an expositional then in a charismatic way to elicit responses from the congregants. New Hope went from ten members in 2000 to two hundred within six months in that same year. His charismatic approach contributed a great deal to the growth of New Hope. However, with all his success through God's guidance, somewhere down the line, he forgot who had exalted him and gifted him to do the works he was doing and somehow lost his way, losing sight of God and what his calling to the ministry was about and causing a significant dissent in the church.

However, the pastor who succeeded him and who still serves as pastor of New Hope came with a seminary education and multiple degrees—accepting the call to pastor a church that had experienced a heartbreaking split from a fallen pastor, which had caused many to leave and look upon the church with disdain. Only twenty members remained. Nonetheless, the new pastor, firmly rooted in expository preaching and teaching, accepted this call from God. In this case, Pastor Spencer has shepherded New Hope for over fifteen years and remains the pastor to this day. Besides, New Hope does not lack sound biblical teaching under his leadership. The pastor teaches sound theological doctrine and foundational expository preaching that pierces the heart. However, many say within the congregation that there is no fire; thus, no growth. There has not been any significant growth for over fifteen years.

Many in the church claim that the Spirit is not moving and that there is no manifestation of the Holy Spirit. Therefore, from their perspective, the church is like dry bones. Although foundational theological doctrines and principles are being preached and taught, this is not enough; they are looking for some spiritual experience. I must confirm that pneumatology (theology of the Holy Spirit) should be preached more from the pulpit. Charismatic preachers, however, are unequivocally acknowledging the Holy Spirit's presence in their preaching, energizing the congregation with charisma and manifesting a euphoria attributed to the Holy Spirit.

From the former to the latter pastor, the two preaching methods used within New Hope show a strong contrast between charismatic and expository preaching. The dissimilarities between these two preaching methods are overwhelming in regard to the responses from congregants. In many cases, expository preaching receives slumber responses from congregants; there is no growth or fiery worship services. However, in contrast, charismatic preaching often results in energetic worship services and tremendous growth. The question remains: Can these two methods of preaching be assimilated and bring glory to the body of Christ (the church) and even to the world in fulfilling the Great Commission?

Statement of the Problem

The problem is that churches grounded foundationally on expository preaching are experiencing a decline in memberships while lacking effective Spirit-filled worship services. These churches are categorically labeled as unhealthy or spiritually dead. New Hope and many other small churches, regardless of denomination, are faced with this dilemma of stagnation regarding numerical growth. Although sound expository preaching and teaching are provided through the men/women of God whom God has called to pastor these churches, there is still no growth.

The Holy Spirit's power manifested through the sound doctrine preached by these pastors—the gospel message's response—yields no growth from a numerical perspective. Although the word is received, congregants are not moved into action, and there is little or no excitement in the worship service. Therefore, from a spiritual perspective, something is missing. This response is not so with charismatic preachers. Pastors who adopt a charismatic delivery method not only move the congregants with their emotional and fiery preaching but experience tremendous growth in their church and ministry and receive unmeasurable prosperity as well. Therefore, this research seeks to understand the charismatic style of preaching and determine if this kind of preaching can be incorporated into a form of expository preaching that is biblically sound

CHAPTER 1: INTRODUCTION

and theologically acceptable as a new movement of the Holy Spirit for the church in this modern age.

The amalgamation of the charismatic and expository preaching styles concerns the hermeneutic issue of aligning with the Holy Spirit's doctrine (pneumatology). However, charismatics are centered on the Holy Spirit's activity with the evidence of speaking in tongues in the believer's life. From this perspective, charismatics view this as the second spiritual experience after conversion. Advocates against the charismatic movement such as Pastor Jerry Vines, whom Mohler quotes in his article, argue from a biblical perspective, not dismissing the movement's significance biblically, because they acknowledge the Bible as authoritative. Despite disagreeing with the movement, Vines gives it credit for its evangelical concern for the ordinary person and for people of all races.[8]

Mohler states that Vines notes that charismatics' openness to all people, which has produced a great harvest, shames many mainline denominations regarding their own approach.[9] Moreover, Vines graciously acknowledges, as Mohler summarizes, "that the majority of charismatics affirm the inerrancy and authority of the Bible and hold to many basic Christian doctrines."[10] However, he disagrees with the charismatic perspective concerning the Spirit's power in the church. Mohler summarizes Vines's approach:

> He rightly points to the emphasis on feelings and experience as the Achilles heel of the Charismatic approach to doctrine and discipleship. "It is vital for Christians to approach the Bible as the final source of authority. There is a tendency today to elevate one's personal experience above truth as revealed in the Bible. Our culture tends to place trust in man's feelings as the prominent feature in making decisions about truth. Our feeling-oriented society wants to go by how it feels about a matter in determining what the truth of a matter is." . . . Vines points to the fundamental truth that the Holy Spirit always exalts Jesus Christ, and never draws center stage

8. Mohler, "Charismatic Movement," para. 7.
9. Mohler, "Charismatic Movement," para. 7.
10. Mohler, "Charismatic Movement," para. 7. These are Mohler's words.

in the biblical revelation. Fully divine, the Holy Spirit is the third person of the Trinity, and many evangelicals err by a lack of recognition of the Holy Spirit's ministry to the church. But the Charismatic movement is based upon an unbiblical presentation of the Spirit's continuing empowerment of the church.[11]

The main issue concerning these two preaching methods is the division between spiritual baptism and the Holy Spirit's activity in individuals' lives within the church. As Mohler explains, "Charismatic and non-charismatic evangelicals are divided on the issue of Spirit baptism Vines insists that both groups believe in the gift of the Holy Spirit to the believer. Nevertheless, the Charismatic believe in a 'baptism of the Spirit' as a second blessing or experience after salvation."[12] Vines argues that it is not biblical and that spiritual baptism happens to all believers "at the moment of salvation," not later.[13]

These issues will be addressed within the scope of this research to determine if these preaching methods can build up the body of Christ and the world. While such approaches are often set in contrast to one another, expository and charismatic preaching concur on core principles of the gospel.

While there is a divide regarding the doctrine of the Spirit, expository preachers and charismatic preachers both acknowledge the Holy Spirit's importance, yet to varying degrees. However, both preaching styles bring forth different results in their worship services. Charismatics invoke the Holy Spirit's empowerment in their worship services, which involves physical manifestations such as being slain in the Spirit, the laying on of hands, and singing. These practices are viewed as unbiblical, because many pastors feel that they ceased with the apostles' passing.

However, the charismatic method of preaching and charismatic practices have yielded a tremendous harvest, as evidenced by their buildings being filled with people and congregants

---

11. Mohler, "Charismatic Movement," paras. 8–9.
12. Mohler, "Charismatic Movement," para. 13.
13. Jerry Vines, qtd. in Mohler, "Charismatic Movement," para. 13.

CHAPTER 1: INTRODUCTION

responding to the pulpit's message. How can these preaching methods be so far apart when both stand on the rock that is Christ? Both ways are relevant and profitable for advancing the gospel, and this research seeks to rectify such a divide and unite both methods of preaching.

Statement of Delimitations

In the research phase, there will be visits to three churches, two fundamentally expository in their preaching style and one charismatic one, to interview the pastor, the chairpersons of the deacon board, and church members after the worship service. Therefore, this will consist of about fifteen people in all. The research process will begin at New Hope Missionary Baptist Church and its congregation. Interviews will then be conducted at other churches in the community grounded in expository and charismatic preaching and worship.

The age group will be those eighteen years and older. The interviews and questionnaires will take place at each church after the service to get input from the pastors, chairpersons of the deacon boards, and members concerning the preaching and the overall worship service. The objective is to gather data on the style of preaching and the worship service overall, and it will solely be my obligation to process this information. The data will be used to evaluate both preaching methods and their effect on the worship service and congregation.

However, the pastor of each church will select the participants. There will be no children under the age of eighteen participating in this research. No names will be given in the interview questionnaire, because it is anonymous.

Statement of Limitations

There will always be limitations in research projects. However, within the scope of this research project, I expect limitations from some congregants. There may be limitations on congregants' truthful insights on their pastor's preaching and the format of their church's worship service. Loyalty to their pastor and church will be a factor in answering the questions, and I have no control concerning that portion of the research.

Besides, some pastors may not want to speak on their preaching style directly, considering that it is a moving of the Spirit that empowers them when delivering the word of God. From this perspective, pastors and ministers are reluctant to divulge their feelings concerning preaching style, which projects holiness when delivering God's word. Although other unforeseen factors may develop within this research project to limit me, however, adjustments are foreseen to ensure that the research's integrity is not compromised. Also, there may be limitations regarding consent from other churches to conduct data gathering, and this will also be out of my control.

Theoretical Basis

Throughout New Testament history, preaching the word of God has been the vehicle through which the "good news of salvation" is revealed. Preaching that Christ is the Son of God, who sacrificed himself for humanity's sins, is the church's foundation in reaching the lost in every corner of this world. From an expository-preaching perspective, this was apparent on the day of Pentecost, when the apostle Peter preached the first sermon that established Christ's church. In Acts 2:17–21, Peter refers to the prophecy of Joel 2:28–32, interpreting these scriptures from the Old Testament that depict Christ, his death, and his resurrection in an expositional way with a charismatic overtone. The movement of God added thousands on the day of Pentecost, because they heard this new but old gospel, which was from the foundations of creation, first to the Jews, then to the gentiles. Charismatics base their movement and preaching method on what happened on the day of Pentecost. The fact that the apostles were empowered by the Holy Spirit to speak in tongues is interpreted by charismatics as confirmation of

CHAPTER 1: INTRODUCTION

them being filled with the Spirit. Therefore, this research intends to explore that theory and determine if there is biblical truth in the charismatics' practice of identifying only those believers who speak in tongues as having the Spirit.

The question at the heart of this research is that which Albert Mohler asks: "Is the Charismatic movement a new wave of the Holy Spirit? How should Christians evaluate the movement, its practices, and its teachings?"[14] From a theological perspective, Peter's first sermon was charismatic and grounded in expository preaching with the Holy Spirit's mighty movement (Acts 2). Therefore, my theological basis is grounded in sound biblical doctrine to determine if these different approaches to preaching can be practiced together biblically.

Charismatic practices and preaching revolve around the work of the Holy Spirit. Charismatic and expository preachers agree on the core of Christian dogma, Christ—the risen Savior, the head of the church—and both hold the same beliefs that set Christianity apart from all other religions. It is in the charismatic movement's interpretation of the Holy Spirit's function in believers' lives that disagreement occurs.

Some people may believe that the preaching and practices of charismatics are unbiblical—that they are walking a thin line into becoming cultlike and misleading believers. What alarms many expository scholars is that charismatics preach from personal feelings concerning the Holy Spirit's work in believers' lives. They emphasize personal experience or feelings above the truth of the gospel.

Charismatics' healing practices of the laying on of hands by the Holy Spirit's power and speaking in tongues are evidence, according to their interpretation, of a subsequent endowment of power from the Holy Spirit. Many advocates against the charismatic movement view this as unbiblical. Nonetheless, many gravitate to this style of preaching and worship. F. B. Meyer asserts, "The one supreme object of the Christian ministry is to preach Christ, and Him Crucified . . . we must never forget that, as its ministers,

14. Mohler, "Charismatic Movement," para. 4.

CHARISMATIC AND EXPOSITORY PREACHING

we have been allowed of God to be trusted with the gospel, and to us has been committed the ministry of Reconciliation."[15] It is incumbent on all believers to stand strong, as our main objective is to preach the gospel. As Paul so graciously asserts in his letter to the brothers and sisters in Philippi:

> It is true that some preach Christ out of envy and rivalry, but others out of goodwill. The latter do so in love, knowing that I am put here for the defense of the gospel. The former preach Christ out of selfish ambition, not sincerely, supposing that they can stir up trouble for me while I am in chains. But what does it matter? The important thing is that in every way, whether from false motives or true, Christ is preached. (Phil 1:15-18)

Paul's assertion here is concise: "But what does it matter? The important thing is that in every way, whether from false motives or true, Christ is preached" (Phil 1:18). Is there sufficient proof to support the claim by expository scholars that charismatics' hermeneutics and homiletics on the Holy Spirit are unbiblical? It is essential to answer this question and determine if the hermeneutical practices and homiletics of the charismatic movement are scriptural and from God's Spirit. Thus, can it be integrated as sound doctrine from an expository viewpoint? Chris Hand provides a profound point of view which is most helpful in this research approach. He asserts:

> Perhaps the most evident legacy today has been the willingness of reformed people to borrow from or imitate certain aspects of the charismatic movement. Those in the middle region of our spectrum who have not rejected the movement outright have at times displayed a pragmatism in adopting elements of the charismatic package. Whatever the discernible flaws that could be seen, however regrettable the teachings, the excesses and . . . odd personalities, these people have felt there was still something to learn.[16]

15. Meyer, *Expository Preaching*, 3.
16. Hand, "Charismatic Movement," 8.

CHAPTER 1: INTRODUCTION

Hand's assertion provides credence to the theory that these two preaching methods can coexist from a preaching and doctrinal perspective. However, biblical support must be at the center, supporting the Scriptures' hermeneutical aspect presented homiletically.

Statement of Methodology

Upon contacting the participating pastors of the churches involved, I will inform them of the context of this research and be a participant by observing the worship service from the pulpit or from within the congregation. After the service, I will present interview questions to the pastors and deacon chairpersons and three members from each congregation. The pastor will ask for the three volunteers to come and fill out the questionnaire. They will be asked a series of questions vital to understanding the individuals' spiritual desires when attending worship services. However, there may be limitations in this analysis, because members may be reluctant to divulge certain spiritual desires.

After service at each church, the interviews will be conducted, getting maximum exposure to the interviewees' worship service and input. All information from interviewees will be confidential and only known by the interviewee and me. All data obtained will be evaluated at New Hope Missionary Baptist Church to see how it can be used to develop an integrated preaching style that can provide growth, practical ministry, and worship service that edifies the body of Christ.

Review of Literature

Expository preaching has been the foundational tool for centuries within the church in conveying the word of God to congregants. However, the rise of the charismatic movement and its preaching has caused great concern among pastors who hold firm to the fundamentals of expository preaching of the Bible.

Charismatic preachers see tremendous growth in their ministries, while in many local churches, pastors who hold steadfastly to expository preaching have experienced a considerable decline in their churches and ministries. Church growth and decline is the primary concern conveyed throughout this research. There are some scholarly journals and books central to this research's development which will support its thesis.

Journal Articles

R. Albert Mohler Jr.'s article "The Charismatic Movement: Cause for Celebration or Concern?" provides strong arguments against this type of preaching and movement; however, Mohler keeps an open mind to God's movement and the Holy Spirit's activity within the charismatic movement's context. He describes the perspective of Pastor Jerry Vines for assistance in analyzing the charismatic movement. For instance, Mohler notes that Vines "acknowledges that the majority of Charismatics affirm the inerrancy and authority of the Bible and hold to many basic Christian doctrines."[17] Vines adamantly opposes the charismatic emphasis on feelings and experience as the basis for their approach to doctrine and discipleship; Vines emphasizes that Christians should "approach the Bible as the final source of authority."[18] Unification is at the core of this research to determine if these two preaching methods can come together to illuminate and grow the church.

In Chris Hand's article "The Legacy of the Charismatic Movement," he provides historical context on how this type of preaching and ministry originated. It is essential for research purposes to understand the origin of the charismatic movement. Chris Hand, being a cessationist, believes that spiritual gifts such as speaking in tongues, prophecy, and healing—which are the very framework of the charismatic doctrine—ceased with the apostolic age. Emphases on the Holy Spirit's baptism, speaking in tongues (glossolalia), and

17. Mohler, "Charismatic Movement," para. 7.
18. Jerry Vines, qtd. in Mohler, "Charismatic Movement," para. 8.

CHAPTER 1: INTRODUCTION

spiritual gifts' full empowerment should be in the church. However, this is where many expository scholars differ in theological thought from charismatics. Being a former charismatic, Pastor Hand provides tremendous insight into the movement's theological understanding of the Scriptures as they are implemented for spiritual consumption leading to spiritual growth.

Perhaps this will help formulate an argument for the best of both worlds (charismatic and expository) in this research. Hand conveys an intriguing admission. He acknowledges, "I can still see the hand of God in the charismatic movement but more as a means for revealing our hearts and refining our convictions than by being a heaven-sent spiritual blessing."[19] Charismatics' defense is grounded in Matt 3:16 and John 1:32–34, where Jesus is baptized and the Holy Spirit comes and remains on him.

Therefore, the charismatic interpretation centers on the Holy Spirit coming down and remaining on him; Jesus, although God in the flesh, was baptized in the Spirit at his baptism and displayed all the spiritual gifts in his ministry. However, advocates against charismatic dogma insist that after the apostles, these gifts ceased. This particular argument is ambiguous, to say the least, because in 1 Cor 12–14, Paul does not say that those gifts ceased to be functional in the church but confirms that they are still a part of the church to be used in ministry. Therefore, how would expository preaching be relevant in conjunction with charismatic dogma on the issue? One must look at the very foundation of expository preaching for the answer.

James F. Stitzinger's journal article "The History of Expository Preaching" provides some substance for sound expository preaching and its place in Christian dogma. Stitzinger conveys:

> Historical study of expository preaching must begin with a proper understanding of the record of preaching in Scripture. Preaching in the Bible is in two primary forms: revelatory preaching and explanatory preaching. All post-biblical preaching has the backdrop of the

---

19. Hand, "Charismatic Movement," 5.

preaching recorded in Scripture and must trace its roots to this source.[20]

Stitzinger provides the foundation for the research to contrast two doctrines from a preaching perspective. He hinges on preaching in two primary forms: revelatory and explanatory preaching. Revelatory preaching is defined as conveying God's revelation to congregants. In contrast, explanatory preaching seeks to explain what is revealed in Scripture. In 2 Tim 2:14–19, Paul tells Timothy to correctly handle the word of truth. Correctly interpreting God's word must draw from both preaching perspectives (charismatic and expository); these principles must be applied to present God's word accurately, even to attempt to find harmony with both preaching doctrines.

Merrill F. Unger's journal article "Expository Preaching" explores the very essence of expository preaching in contrast to the position of charismatic preaching as it pertains to the church and Scripture. Unger's article argues that the preacher's principal task is to proclaim the truth set in the Old and New Testaments.[21] Unger asserts that all preaching must be sound doctrine, because it is the duty of any preacher of God's word, charismatic or expository, to hold the same platform in the church's pulpit.

Like Paul in 2 Tim 4:2, Unger's call is to preach the word. Although many disagree with the charismatic interpretations of Scripture, researching some avenues in which the charismatic doctrine of preaching holds some sound theological ground in its hermeneutical approach to Scripture could help their argument.

Books

In his book *He Expounded: A Guide to Expository Preaching*,[22] author Douglas M. White considers the necessity of sound Bible preaching to enrich Christians' lives in the local churches. As

---

20. Stitzinger, "History of Expository Preaching," 7.
21. Unger, "Expository Preaching," 332.
22. White, *He Expounded*.

CHAPTER 1: INTRODUCTION

Paul asserts in Phil 3:15, "All of us, then, who are mature should take such a view of things. And if on some point you think differently, that too God will make clear to you." The objective of this research is to find common ground between two preaching methods that can move and mature the believer and bring them closer to Christ in harmony.

D. A. Carson's book *Showing the Spirit: A Theological Exposition of 1 Corinthians 12–14* attempts to clarify what Paul was asserting concerning spiritual gifts in his epistle to the Christians in Corinth. Carson contrasts Paul's assertions concerning spiritual gifts with charismatics' interpretation of 1 Cor 12–14. From Carson's perspective, according to his interpretation of Paul's letter to the believers in Corinth, every Christian is charismatic.[23] Christians, by the power of the Holy Spirit, will display charisma regardless of method—be it expository or charismatic—because the gifts of the Spirit are active in the church for ministry. His perspective will be valuable in this research regarding charismatic and expository preaching.

Gordon D. Fee's commentary *The First Epistle to the Corinthians*[24] provides analysis and insight into Paul's letter to the church in Corinth, elucidating the Spirit's gifts and how charismatics interpret it to formulate their doctrine and movement regarding the church. If this research can determine a concise interpretation of 1 Corinthians and the theology of charismatic dogma and sound expository preaching, perhaps the two preaching methods can be integrated to help with church growth at local levels.

Richard B. Gaffin Jr.'s book *Perspectives on Pentecost: New Testament Teaching on the Gifts of the Holy Spirit*[25] contributes to this research by exploring the New Testament teachings on the gifts of the Holy Spirit. It will help me evaluate the teachings on spiritual gifts from the charismatic and expository viewpoints, from the Synoptic Gospels to Revelation.

---

23. Carson, *Showing the Spirit*, 21.
24. Fee, *First Epistle*.
25. Gaffin, *Perspectives on Pentecost*.

John F. MacArthur Jr.'s book *Charismatic Chaos* conveys strong opposition against the charismatic movement as being close to cultic in their doctrine. MacArthur asserts, "Most charismatics, if they are honest with themselves, would have to acknowledge that personal experience and not Scripture is the foundation of their belief system."[26] Acts 2:4, which states that on the day of Pentecost, all were filled with the Spirit, is the core truth for charismatic doctrine and preaching of the New Testament. Understanding the charismatic approach and interpretation of Scripture is essential for this research to contrast both preaching principles.

Authors Rich Nathan and Ken Wilson, in their book *Empowered Evangelicals: Bringing Together the Best of the Evangelical and Charismatic Worlds*,[27] seek to convey the positive elements about charismatic dogma. This literature is at the core of the research, which will bring both worlds together, revealing some parallels between the two methods. From my perspective, both charismatic and expository preaching can be integrated to form sound doctrine. There are solid arguments for Scripture's charismatic position that can harmonize with sound expository doctrine if approached with specific hermeneutical skills and sound homiletics. In 1 Cor 14:26–33, Paul alludes to the fact that spiritual gifts are meant to strengthen the church and not weaken it.

Jean-Jacques Suurmond's book *Word and Spirit at Play: Towards a Charismatic Theology*[28] brings perspective on charismatic theology, which has credence in some cases from a hermeneutical approach. However, this research will analytically probe the author's thoughts and arguments on his charismatic theological position and its interpretation of Scripture.

Thomas D. Lea and David Alan Black's book *The New Testament: Its Background and Message* will contribute from an analytical perspective on the charismatic interpretation of spiritual gifts in 1 Cor 12:1–11 that formulates their theological doctrine.

26. MacArthur, *Charismatic Chaos*, 23.
27. Nathan and Wilson, *Empowered Evangelicals*.
28. Suurmond, *Word and Spirit*.

CHAPTER 1: INTRODUCTION

The authors assert, "Paul's instructions were designed to correct the abuses the Corinthians allowed within the church."[29] This passage of Scripture seems to be at the core of debate concerning charismatic doctrine. However, if this can be addressed from a sound expository approach concerning spiritual gifts, both preaching methods would benefit the church. From an informative way that allows the Holy Spirit to do what the Lord sent him to do, there can be harmony with these preaching methods.

Elmer L. Towns's book *A Journey Through the New Testament* provides a survey of the New Testament for this thesis project, which will be beneficial in drawing parallels and contrasts between charismatic and expository interpretations of the New Testament, especially the book of Acts and 1 Cor 12–14.

Walter A. Elwell's *Evangelical Dictionary of Theology*[30] contributes to this project's insight into the charismatic movement's religious nature and its theological thoughts that formulate their doctrine, church implementation, and how it affects the congregants in worship service.

William W. Klein, Craig L. Blomberg, and Robert L. Hubbard Jr. produced the book *Introduction to Biblical Interpretation*,[31] which will help me analyze both charismatic and expository doctrine interpretations from a hermeneutical approach.

As stated, the purpose of this research is to determine if these two preaching methods are a movement of the Spirit and God's will. Also, another purpose is to articulate whether these two theological thoughts and doctrines can work together as sound doctrine for the church's edification and growth, especially at the local church level. The interpretations by the charismatic movement concerning the doctrine of the Holy Spirit and gifts of the Spirit are at the heart of the question that divides the two. Most scholars agree that charismatics hold to the Christian dogma that the Scriptures have authority first and foremost in the church and their lives.

---

29. Lea and Black, *New Testament*, 414.
30. Elwell, *Evangelical Dictionary*.
31. Klein et al., *Biblical Interpretation*.

CHARISMATIC AND EXPOSITORY PREACHING

Kilian McDonnell's book *Charismatic Renewal and the Churches* presents a detailed look into the church's charismatic Pentecostal movement. He examines the movement from a historical, sociological, cultural, anthropological, psychological, and theological perspective.[32] However, his approach is not theological in content; his objective is to respond to the charismatic Pentecostal movement. This research will draw heavily from chapter 1 of the book, "Human Experience and Religious Meaning," which concerns the charismatic movement and its preaching method.

John F. MacArthur Jr.'s book *The Charismatics* explores the charismatic movement in depth. Not only does he analyze the errors of the charismatic movement's dogma from a biblical perspective but he also acknowledges that the movement's foundation is based on an experience that transcends all denominational lines.[33] MacArthur asserts, "In the Charismatic movement there is a certain commonality based, not upon theology, but upon the experience of being 'baptized in the Holy Spirit' and usually speaking in tongues."[34] MacArthur's analysis of the charismatic doctrine contributes to this research the analytical basis of understanding charismatic preaching methods.

Scripture References

> Don't you know that you yourselves are God's temple and that God's Spirit dwells in your midst? If anyone destroys God's temple, God will destroy that person; for God's temple is sacred, and you together are that temple. (1 Cor 3:16–17)

This Scripture is preached from expository and charismatic pulpits throughout the world. Charismatics argue that a believer must experience the Holy Spirit's baptism as evidence of having

---

32. McDonnell, *Charismatic Renewal*, ix.
33. MacArthur, *Charismatics*, 13.
34. MacArthur, *Charismatics*, 13.

CHAPTER 1: INTRODUCTION

the Spirit. However, as Paul asserts in verses 16–17: "You are the temple, and the Spirit lives in you."

First Corinthians 12–14 are the chapters on which the charismatic movement builds 90 percent of their doctrine concerning spiritual gifts and the Holy Spirit. From their perspective, these spiritual gifts are still active in the church today, as it was with the early church and the apostles.

In 1 Cor 12:1–11, Paul affirms the gifts of the Spirit. Christians have been given spiritual gifts by the Holy Spirit to be utilized in the body of Christ (the church). Paul did not dismiss the usage of spiritual gifts in the church at Corinth but used the gifts responsibly to edify the body of Christ. However, expository and charismatic preachers expound on this passage to conclude that spiritual gifts are present in the ecclesia. First Corinthians 14:26–33 states:

> What then shall we say, brothers? When you come together, everyone has a hymn, or a word of instruction, a revelation, a tongue, or an interpretation. All of these must be done for the strengthening of the church. If anyone speaks in a tongue, two or at the most three should speak, one at a time, and someone must interpret. If there is no interpreter, the speaker should keep quiet in the church and speak to himself and God. Two or three prophets should speak, and the others should weigh carefully what is said. And if a revelation comes to someone who is sitting down, the first speaker should stop. For you can all prophesy in turn so that everyone may be instructed and encouraged. The spirits of prophets are subject to the control of prophets. For God is not of disorder but of peace.

Here, Paul is instructing the believers in Corinth on how to utilize their gifts in orderly worship. One cannot dispute Paul's intentions here, because from verses 26 to 33, he is concise in how believers should conduct themselves in orderly worship when utilizing the Spirit's gifts. He further seals it in verse 33, stating, "God is not a God of disorder but of peace." Charismatics point to this passage of Scripture to confirm glossolalia usage (speaking in tongues) and prophesy in the ecclesia.

CHARISMATIC AND EXPOSITORY PREACHING

Matthew 3:16: "As soon as Jesus was baptized, he went up out of the water. At that moment, heaven was opened, and he saw the Spirit of God descending like a dove and lighting on him." Matthew is conveying to Christians that even Jesus, submitting to baptism, received the Holy Spirit at that time and not as a subsequent event, as charismatics advocate that believers will experience. The Holy Spirit is active at the moment of the believer's conversion. From this perspective, it is essential for expositional preaching to convey the word of truth rightly.

In 2 Tim 2:14–19, Paul urges Timothy to correctly handle the word of truth. Correctly interpreting God's word involves drawing from both preaching perspectives. Paul asserts, "Do your best to present yourself to God as one approved, a workman who does not need to be ashamed and who correctly handles the word of truth" (2 Tim 2:15). Paul gave Timothy this charge to keep him on that narrow path of preaching the truth of God's word among false teachers leading astray his flock, and this holds to every preacher that preaches the gospel. As Lea and Black assert, Paul directed Timothy to respond to errors by avoiding contentious debates and teaching the truth to those false teachers willing to listen.[35] Therefore, expository preachers should take this same course of action in dealing with the charismatic's errors in Scripture from an expository position.

Second Timothy 4:2–3 states: "Preach the Word; be prepared in season and out of season; correct, rebuke and encourage with great patience and careful instruction. For the time will come when men will not put up with sound doctrine. Instead, to suit their desires, they will gather around them a great number of teachers to say what their itching ears want to hear." Advocates against the charismatic movement and its preaching invoke this passage to argue against much of charismatic preaching doctrine. Some brand the charismatic movement as a cult and accuse them of using God's word for personal gain and control over the congregation, just as Paul, in Phil 1:15–18, describes how some misuse the gospel for their gain and for other reasons as well:

---

35. Lea and Black, *New Testament*, 484.

CHAPTER 1: INTRODUCTION

> It is true that some preach Christ out of envy and rivalry, but others out of goodwill. The latter do so in love, knowing that I am put here for the defense of the gospel. The former preach Christ out of selfish ambition, not sincerely, supposing that they can stir up trouble for me while I am in chains. But what does it matter? The important thing is that in every way, whether from false motives or true, Christ is preached. And because of this, I rejoice. (Phil 1:15–18)

Philippians 1:15–18 provides a foundation for contrasting the methods and motives of expository and charismatic preachers, and for understanding why charismatics and expository preachers have chosen their form of preaching to convey the gospel. Paul is clear that some are preaching with a particular motive in mind. Charismatic preachers have been scrutinized concerning their preaching methods and the doctrine they preach.

Philippians 3:15 states: "All of us, then, who are mature should take such a view of things. And if on some point you think differently, that too God will make clear to you." Paul is conveying that every believer's purpose and goal should be to focus on the things of God. Keeping the focus on Christ and spreading the gospel as mandated is the goal of the church. If there should arise some difference in thinking, trust that God will make it clear.

This research aims to find the common ground of these different preaching styles to solidify the methods if possible. When analyzing expository and charismatic preaching methods, there must be some commonality in how they agree on Scripture interpretation. Preaching is the central part of church ministry, which makes this research significant, because God has called certain individuals to proclaim his word, and they must preach the truth without adding or taking away from it regardless of their preaching methods, be it charismatic or expository.

The commonality of both preaching methods, to start with, is the Holy Spirit, who anoints and empowers the preacher to proclaim God's word. Without the Holy Spirit's endowment of divine power, words spoken from the pulpit are just that, words spoken from human effort. Both methods of preaching must yield to the guidance of the Holy Spirit and be empowered to preach God's word, which will prick the hearts of the saved and unsaved that they may come to Christ and receive salvation and the love that Christ gives. Greg Heisler makes a very profound point concerning the definition of preaching. He states:

> One of the most obvious omissions of the Spirit's role in preaching is seen in how rare it is to find the Spirit incorporated into a definition of preaching. This is ironic since the way you define something will ultimately determine the outcome you can expect. In general, preaching definitions tend to center on the preacher, the Bible, and the delivery. Yet, if preaching is the Spirit's ministry and if the final goal of our preaching is a demonstration of the Spirit's power, then we must define preaching to encompass the rich theology of Word and Spirit from the beginning.[36]

---

36. Heisler, *Spirit-Led Preaching*, 11.

Chapter 2: Expository and Charismatic Preaching

What are expository and charismatic preaching? First, the concept of preaching must be understood from the foundation of Christian dogma, which proclaims that the Bible is the word of God given to man by divine inspiration of the Holy Spirit (God breathed). Walter A. Elwell's *Evangelical Dictionary of Theology* defines preaching in four ways: (1) "Preaching is the communication of truth through personality"; (2) "Preaching is the manifestation of the incarnate Word from the written word through the spoken word"; (3) "Preaching is the truth mediated through personality to constrain conscience at once"; and (4) "Preaching is the divine truth voiced by a chosen personality to meet human need."[1] Semantically, these definitions define the concept of preaching. However, for research purposes, the first definition ("Preaching is the communication of truth through personality") serves to be the most prudent approach regarding expository and charismatic preaching styles/methods (note, those empowered by the Holy Spirit). However, it should be noted that the primary duty of any preacher is preparing and delivering sermons.[2] This chapter will delve into the differences between these two preaching methods.

Preaching is the catalyst by which the gospel is revealed to the world, but these two preaching methods harbor different congregations and produce different results. Charismatic preaching excites those in attendance, while expository preaching without

1. Elwell, *Evangelical Dictionary*, 948.
2. Ray, *Expository Preaching*, 13.

25

the element of charisma seems to fall on deaf ears—considering that both preach the same gospel but from a different approach and perspective. In chapter 2, we will explore both methods and the preaching styles of expository and charismatic preaching. For the sake of the gospel, it is incumbent that preaching be at the forefront of advancing God's word to a depraved world. Jesus is concise concerning his mandate to his disciples in Matt 28:19–20: "Therefore, go and make disciples of all nations, baptizing them in the name of the father and of the Son and the Holy Spirit, and teaching them to obey everything I have commanded you." The preaching of the gospel is the bridge that connects God's word to the world; proclamation requires a response from people in attendance, the saved and unsaved alike. Paul solidifies this position with his letter to the believers in Romans. He asserts in Rom 10:14–15: "How then, can they call on the one they have not believed in? And how can they believe in the one of whom they have not heard? And how can they hear without someone preaching to them? And how can they preach unless they are sent?"

Understanding the concept of preaching and its importance to the foundation of Christian dogma is essential to advancing the gospel. Preaching under the Holy Spirit's unction gravitates people toward the church and leads them to accept Christ as Lord and Savior. Therefore, analyzing these two preaching methods from a hermeneutical perspective reveals that the differences are in their interpretation of Scripture and delivery of the text preached, although both forms of preaching hold to the authority of Scripture. Charismatics believe in utilizing the spiritual gifts found in 1 Cor 12. However, expository preaching stands on the exegesis, hermeneutics, and homiletics of Scripture. Expository preaching searches the very depths of the Scriptures, bringing forth an oasis of truths concerning God's word. Both preaching methods will be evaluated for research purposes, leading to a concise understanding of both methods.

CHAPTER 2: EXPOSITORY AND CHARISMATIC PREACHING

Expository Preaching

F. B. Meyer defines expository preaching as "the consecutive treatment of some book or extended portion of Scripture on which the preacher has concentrated head and heart, brain and brawn, over which he has thought and wept and prayed until it has yielded up its inner secret, and the spirit of it has passed into his spirit."[3] The rigorous work of preparing a sermon is most rewarding when the preparer has labored over the text and the Spirit of God has revealed certain truths to be conveyed to the church and the world. When the man or woman of God steps to the pulpit to deliver God's word, the author's original intent must be revealed. Expository preaching is a hermeneutical/homiletical exposition that seeks to interpret, intelligently amplify, and accurately and effectively apply a Scripture passage.[4] There are tremendous advantages to expository preaching that will edify the body of Christ. From an apologetic perspective, expository preaching defends Christianity from all advocates against God's word (the Bible). There are some varieties of expository preaching: (1) "exegetical exposition," (2) "doctrinal exposition," (3) "historical exposition," (4) "biographical exposition," and (5) "character exposition."[5] These five variations of expository preaching can, if carefully constructed, be delivered in one expositional sermon.

Concerning expository preaching, Faris D. Whitesell, in his book *Power in Expository Preaching*, notes:

> In the expository approach, we study not only the roots, trunk, and branches of our tree; we also consider its leaves, soil, climate, inner ring system, distinctive features, life history, and relation to other trees and vegetation around it; the uses to which we can put this tree, and how to reproduce this tree and others like it not only here but in other parts of the world. In other words, we seek a comprehensive, detailed, and thorough knowledge of our tree. From the mass of information

---

3. Meyer, *Expository Preaching*, 29.
4. Ray, *Expository Preaching*, 47.
5. Ray, *Expository Preaching*, 59–67.

that we compile, we arrange our expository talk about our tree. We find a subject, a theme, a thesis, a logical outline, and a sound development. We may not use all the material we have gathered, but we use most of it. This is the expository method.[6]

What is unique about expository preaching is that it takes its audience on a textual journey, revealing the text's historical, biographical, doctrinal, and exegetical exposition when fully applied. There is tremendous power in expository preaching. It opens Scripture and the author's fundamental truths to the audience and then applies it to the modern era for the church and the world to digest. There are tremendous advantages to expository preaching. For instance, when applied correctly, expository preachers provide a candid view of the author's original intent at that time in history—revealing certain truths that will benefit the body of Christ. However, if the expository preacher does not convey God's word with power from the Spirit, it may not resonate with the congregation, which may result in the congregation missing out on the richness of expository preaching. Pastors that preach from an interpretive (expository) approach yield no growth in their churches; even with sound doctrine, this could result from a lack of charisma. Compared with pastors preaching charismatically, expository preaching appears dry, regardless of how informative the message is. Without the Holy Spirit's movement, it will lack divine power to penetrate the hearts of those who hear the good news of the gospel.

Therefore, why are charismatic preaching pastors experiencing unspeakable success and church growth compared to expository-preaching pastors? How could this be when both preaching methods come under the unction of the Holy Spirit? This issue will be discussed later in this chapter. Nonetheless, there is insurmountable power in expository preaching that convicts the soul and humbles the heart even if the word is not conveyed with charisma. The Holy Spirit confirms the words spoken by those whom God has called to preach his word, regardless of preaching

6. Whitesell, *Power in Expository Preaching*, xiv.

CHAPTER 2: EXPOSITORY AND CHARISMATIC PREACHING

approach. It is the Holy Spirit's anointing that saturates the servant of God when preaching. Charismatic or expository preachers must be anointed, because "the anointing is the special presence of the Holy Spirit in the life and ministry of God's servant, which produces an inspiring awareness of the divine presence."[7] Even with God's anointing, preparations must be done; this is what makes expository preachers so unique in their expositional approach in preparing a sermon—knowing all there is to know about a particular passage of Scripture and even their audience.

Therefore, it is incumbent on the preacher to know his audience, their age range, educational range, occupations, cultural interests, prejudices, gender distribution, and spiritual maturity to be more effective when delivering God's word.[8] Being prepared is essential, but ultimately, the Holy Spirit and his anointing is the power behind all preaching. As Paul admonished Timothy in 2 Tim 4:2–3, "Preach the word; be prepared in season and out of season; correct, rebuke and encourage—with great patience and careful instruction. For the time will come when people will not put up with sound doctrine. Instead, to suit their own desires, they will gather around them a great number of teachers to say what their itching ears want to hear." That is why expository preaching for many pastors is the most fundamental approach in conveying God's word to his people, regardless of whether some people may not adhere to it for whatever reason, and why these pastors continue to preach the unadulterated word of God. Preaching the word is God's way of transforming a culture that is plagued by misdirected love, a culture that doesn't realize it is in darkness and far from God.[9]

---

7. Forbes, *Holy Spirit & Preaching*, 54.
8. Whitesell, *Power in Expository Preaching*, 68.
9. Orrick et al., *Encountering God*, 32.

Expository Preaching Provides Authority and Power

According to Merrill F. Unger, expository preaching is, in fact, biblical preaching.[10] It is the preaching of God's unadulterated word from the beginning to the end of every sermon. Unger asserts:

> Expository preaching is first and foremost biblical preaching. It is emphatically not preaching about the Bible but preaching the Bible. "What saith the Lord" is the alpha and the omega of expository preaching. It begins in the Bible and ends in the Bible, and all that intervenes springs from the Bible. In other words, expository preaching is Bible-centered preaching. Whatever extra-biblical material is employed, illustrations from human experience, history, archeology, philosophy, art, or science must be purely subsidiary and strictly fitted into one single aim to elucidate the portion of Scripture chosen, whatever its length, and enforce its claims upon hearers.[11]

Expository preaching's power and authority is that the preacher reveals the Bible's teachings and content concisely to the audience.[12] Pastors are equipped to teach Scripture in season and out of season. They should correctly handle the word of truth. When the preacher, with the power of the Spirit, concisely explains the meaning of a particular passage of Scripture and effectively reveals its truths to his audience, then we see expository preaching at its best.[13] It must be noted that even charismatic preaching stands before this very light as well. Therefore, both preaching methods (expository and charismatic) are on common expositional grounds. The power of God's word is life changing, cutting deep into the hearts of humanity, bringing about a change in the individual who yields to the word by the power of the Holy Spirit, revealing the love of Christ in their lives.

---

10. Unger, "Expository Preaching," 333.
11. Unger, "Expository Preaching," 333.
12. Unger, "Expository Preaching," 333.
13. Unger, "Expository Preaching," 334.

CHAPTER 2: EXPOSITORY AND CHARISMATIC PREACHING

Expository Preaching Is Preaching a Revelatory Truth

The preacher who embraces expository preaching must labor more than any other in preparation for a sermon, because this preacher searches the Scriptures rigorously to ensure that what is being preached is accurate. The preacher must reveal to the congregation God's revelatory truth. William W. Klein notes the importance of one's approach:

> The view of the nature of the Bible that an interpreter holds will determine what meaning that interpreter will find in it. If the Bible owes its origin to an all-powerful divine being who has revealed his message via human writers, then the objective of interpretation will be to understand the meaning communicated through the divinely inspired document. If the interpreter adopts an alternative explanation of the Bible's origin, then he or she will prescribe other goals in interpreting the text. We adopt the presupposition that the Bible is a supernatural book, God's written revelation to his people given through prepared and selected spokespersons by the process of inspiration. This has been the church's universal creed throughout its history.[14]

The sole purpose of an expository preacher is to make clear the word of God and to reveal its biblical truths as God inspired them through his agents. God's purpose through Scripture was to reveal himself to his creation, to correct what went wrong in the beginning with man's fall into sin, and to provide a vehicle for man to be reconciled back to him and obtain salvation. Therefore, the expository preacher must reveal Scripture's clarity in that the things necessary for salvation can be understood from the Bible without special techniques or higher education.[15] James Forbes correctly asserts, "It is the anointing of the Holy Spirit that helps the preacher understand and prepare for the ministry

---

14. Klein et al., *Biblical Interpretation*, 143–44.
15. Olford and Olford, *Anointed Expository Preaching*, 71.

of the Word . . . the Spirit will make the difference between our failure and our fulfillment."[16]

Suppose Forbes is correct in his assertion that the Holy Spirit's work helps the preacher understand and present the word of God. In that case, there is no differentiation in preparation between expository and charismatic preachers. Because there is only one Spirit (God's Spirit) that dwells in all believers, expository and charismatic preachers are connected by this one Spirit, who alone can reveal God's truth. However, it is a matter of interpretation of specific passages in question, distinguishing or dividing the two preaching methods. Arguably, it is the utilization of spiritual gifts when preaching that sets them apart. When comparing the two preaching styles, the charismatic usage of the Spirit's gifts arouses the congregation, bringing them into worship and awe of God. Although people hear the word in understandable terms from an interpretive approach, people still need to see God's power in action.

People desire and even crave the church's supernatural movement; this is why charismatic preaching has attracted many people to the church. Although there has been a decline over the years in the church, charismatic churches seem to maintain large membership, at least from my observation from visiting expository and charismatic churches in the past. With the speaking in tongues, laying on of hands, and being slain in the Spirit, charismatic preachers keep their congregation in awe of God from a spiritual-experience perspective. However, is the charismatic preacher's spiritual-experience approach of preaching biblical and in harmony with God's word? The charismatic movement must be evaluated and researched from a theological and biblical perspective to answer this question. Surprisingly, many Christians think that the charismatic movement lacks biblical support but is reluctant to state this publicly.[17]

---

16. Forbes, *Holy Spirit & Preaching*, 71.
17. MacArthur, *Charismatic Chaos*, 13.

CHAPTER 2: EXPOSITORY AND CHARISMATIC PREACHING

Charismatic Preaching

Charismatic preaching and its movement have set the twenty-first century ablaze with their preaching approach to ministry and doctrinal teachings. Charismatic preachers seem to have such an anointing on their lives, preaching, and ministry, leaving people amazed and drawing thousands if not millions into the church and ministries. Many invoke the Holy Spirit as the agent leading and guiding their preaching and other events that may occur during the worship service—giving the congregation a spiritual experience that leaves them wanting more from that experience. However, I concur with Dr. Kenny McComas:

> We live in a day of counterfeits and synthetics. From plastics and Styrofoam, everything from artificial fruit to artificial building beams is being made. Wax museums display human duplications so lifelike, it's difficult to recognize with a casual glance they are only a figurine. Unfortunately, our day is also a day of political racketeers and religious phonies. People who have pawned themselves off on the masses as Spirit-filled, divinely-directed people are nothing more than emissaries of Satan. They have been found out to be alcoholics, dope addicts, operators of prostitution rings, and involved in all sorts of immoral acts. Many have been proven to be professional play actors prying upon the sympathy of sincere people. Since it's so difficult to judge a book by its cover, many mis-judgments have been made. "God looketh on the heart but man looketh on the outward appearance." Jesus gave us the blue and red litmus paper, however, enabling us to run a spiritual test and avoid being taken in. "By this shall all men know," said our lovely Lord in John 13:35. "Ye shall know them by their fruit," Matthew 7:16.[18]

Charismatic preaching is mesmerizing, and one can see it as a spiritual movement of God if the charismatic preacher holds to the very foundation of expository preaching, which is God's revelation to his creation. God's word (Scripture) is inerrant; thus, the Bible's

---

18. McComas, *Charismatic Corinthians*, 1.

CHARISMATIC AND EXPOSITORY PREACHING

authority is the foundation of Christian doctrine.[19] However, there is a divide in specific interpretations of scriptures concerning charismatic theology and teachings—especially the charismatic interpretation of 1 Cor. 12:7–11 concerning the gifts of the Spirit.

Charismatic theology stands on this passage, where Paul acknowledges that the gifts of the Spirit are there in the church. From this perspective, charismatics are adherents of the belief that the gifts of the Spirit are still active in the modern church, as they were in the earlier church. No one can deny that the Holy Spirit must be involved in Christ's church. In John 14:15–21 and 16:5–16, Jesus clarifies the mission of the Holy Spirit before going to the cross. Jesus states that the Father will give the disciples the Holy Spirit, who will be with them forever (John 14:16), and lays out the work of the Spirit in John 16:5–16. However, advocates against charismatic doctrine would argue that Jesus is only speaking to the disciples in this text, because the church had not come to fruition. Nonetheless, the charismatic doctrine is formulated from scriptures such as these particular passages.

Charismatic Movement

As stated in the former chapter, the charismatic movement "is one of the most remarkable developments of the twentieth [and twenty-first]" centuries.[20] Starting from "modest beginnings in the Azusa Street revival," the charismatic movement has become "the fastest-growing segment of Christianity" in the US and globally.[21] The charismatic movement has drawn millions, creating megachurches throughout the US and worldwide. There are many factions of Christianity in this movement: traditional Pentecostals, the Assemblies of God, and the Vineyard Movement.[22]

---

19. Mohler, "Charismatic Movement," paras. 7–8. Here, Mohler is summarizing and agreeing with Pastor Jerry Vines's perspective.
20. Mohler, "Charismatic Movement," para. 1.
21. Mohler, "Charismatic Movement," para. 1.
22. Mohler, "Charismatic Movement," para. 2.

CHAPTER 2: EXPOSITORY AND CHARISMATIC PREACHING

Charismatic influence has penetrated most traditional denominations, such as Episcopalians in the United States, Anglicans worldwide, Roman Catholics, and Baptists.[23] According to Mohler, "Central to the movement is the claim that a new visitation of the Holy Spirit has brought back the apostolic gifts and manifestations of the New Testament."[24] With an emphasis on a second blessing after conversion, Mohler asks, "Is the Charismatic movement a new wave of the Holy Spirit? How should Christians evaluate the movement, its practices, and its teachings?"[25]

This research project aims to answer these questions and more concerning the charismatic phenomena from a preaching and biblical perspective and regarding doctrinal teachings. It also aims to understand why its preaching methods are effective in terms of Christian growth in the church compared to expository preaching. Therefore, to grasp charismatic preaching, one must first evaluate the movement's theological and biblical concepts. Robert H. Culpepper notes:

> The charismatic movement is an interdenominational movement within Christendom seeking to promote personal and church renewal and recovery of spiritual power by an emphasis upon the exercise of the gifts of the Spirit mentioned by Paul in 1 Corinthians 12:7-11. Historically, the movement is related to Pentecostalism, but it is not a separatist movement exercised in isolation from the rest of Christendom. Rather, it is Pentecostalism penetrating the various denominations of the Christian church, Protestant and Catholic. Generally speaking, the charismatic movement, instead of encouraging those who come under its influence to form a new Pentecostal denomination or to join an already existing one, urges its adherents to remain within their own churches and denominations and to act as spiritual leaven within them.[26]

---

23. Mohler, "Charismatic Movement," para. 3.
24. Mohler, "Charismatic Movement," para. 2.
25. Mohler, "Charismatic Movement," para. 4.
26. Culpepper, *Charismatic Movement*, 10.

Culpepper's view of the charismatic movement is historically related to Pentecostalism and not a separate movement within itself, because its roots are profoundly connected to Pentecostalism and have infiltrated many denominations, especially in the Baptist churches. The charismatic influence within the Baptist churches is not antagonistic but has enhanced the Baptist churches' worship services. According to James D. Berkley, there are charismatic churches within other denominations, mixing both a liturgical and charismatic worship style, thus enhancing the service.[27] Berkley defines "charismatic" as "the anglicized rendering for gifts of the Holy Spirit. Here the very word charismatic declares the openness of the worshipper to both receive gifts and to minister them to others [1 Pet 4:10]."[28] Many charismatics seek the presence of God and desire that spiritual experience that only the Holy Spirit can provide in their lives. However, this pursuit of God's presence can be misleading and perceived as overly emotional and without substance for those unfamiliar with charismatic worship.[29]

Theological Issues with the Charismatic Movement

Many theologians concur with Culpepper and Berkley's analysis of the charismatic movement. Many believers within the traditional denominations embrace charismatic views. Believers on Sunday mornings enter their place of worship, needing to see some manifestation of God's Spirit in the church and their lives. Many believers, regardless of denomination, desire the Holy Spirit's movement in their lives. Culpepper is right in his assertion that all Christians have the gift (charisma) of eternal life, as Paul states in Rom 6:23, and that every believer is given the gift of the Holy Spirit, who belongs to Christ (Acts 2:38, Rom 8:9).[30] From a theological perspective, according to Culpepper:

---

27. Berkley, *Leadership Handbook*, 153.
28. Berkley, *Leadership Handbook*, 152.
29. Berkley, *Leadership Handbook*, 152.
30. Culpepper, *Charismatic Movement*, 11.

CHAPTER 2: EXPOSITORY AND CHARISMATIC PREACHING

Charismatics adhere to basic Christian theology, such as is expressed in the Apostles' Creed, as well as to the particular teachings of their own churches and denominations. In addition to these, normally they have some distinctive doctrines which are related to their charismatic experience. Most leaders of the charismatic movement claim to ground such doctrinal views, not on their experience but on the teachings of Holy Scripture. They insist that in all cases, Scripture provides the norms. They believe that the interpretation of Scripture should not be weakened in order to conform to contemporary experience; instead, contemporary Christian experience should be blessed and empowered until it conforms to the pattern of Scripture.[31]

Charismatics believe and preach that the power of the Holy Spirit is the power of the church. That brings about spiritual energy to be used by the church in carrying out the Great Commission. Charismatics argue that the tremendous power that the early church demonstrated is missing in most churches and Christians today.[32] This ideology is derived from their interpretations of the Scriptures. From the charismatic's theological viewpoint, churches today reside in elegant buildings and have beautiful liturgies and a variety of professional ministers but lack what the early church possessed, "Spiritual Power."[33] Charismatics present a strong argument for the spiritual power or lack thereof in churches today. From the charismatic spiritual point of view, the Holy Spirit's power bestowed upon the early church is still there for the modern church to utilize.

Their theological reasoning is that the Holy Spirit in the early church endowed the church with spiritual powers in the early church to heal the sick, speak in tongues, cast out demons, make the lame walk, and make the deaf hear—and even, in some cases, to raise the dead (see Acts 5:12–16, 20:7–12). Their assertion is in agreement with Scripture's argument that the same spiritual

---

31. Culpepper, *Charismatic Movement*, 53.
32. Culpepper, *Charismatic Movement*, 53.
33. Culpepper, *Charismatic Movement*, 54.

power is still available for the church to use in this modern age. Charismatics also point out that Christians in the early church experienced God moving in response to their prayers, that miracles attended prayer, and that the Holy Spirit empowered the word being preached.[34] As Culpepper states:

> The church on the day of Pentecost provoked from the crowd's reactions of amazement and perplexity. People may possibly be perplexed at the church today, but they are seldom amazed at what is happening because the wonder and sparkle of those early days is usually missing. But the charismatic ask[s], why should it be so? Does not the New Testament tell us that Jesus Christ is the same yesterday and today and forever (Heb. 13:8)? And does not Jesus promise his disciples, "He who believes in me will also do the work that I do, and greater works than these will he do because I go to the father" (John 14:12)? The New Testament associates spiritual power with the work of the Holy Spirit. All power has been delivered to the risen Lord in heaven and on earth (Matthew 28:18), and he pours [it] out on the disciples through the Holy Spirit (Acts 1:8; 2:33; 4:31). Paul can say that his words and deeds were attended "by the power of signs and wonders, by the power of the Holy Spirit" (Romans 15:19; cf. 1 Cor. 2:4). He reminds the Galatians that by hearing with faith, God supplies the Spirit to them and works miracles (Gal. 3:5). Obviously, what is lacking in the church today, say the charismatics, is the same kind of experience of the Holy Spirit, which the early church had.[35]

Charismatics' preaching and theological teachings are based upon the Scriptures noted by Culpepper. Their theological premise for what they believe is the rediscovery of what the New Testament calls baptism in or with the Holy Spirit, which is viewed as the Pentecostal experience—receiving the Holy Spirit, which endows

---

34. Culpepper, *Charismatic Movement*, 54.
35. Culpepper, *Charismatic Movement*, 54.

CHAPTER 2: EXPOSITORY AND CHARISMATIC PREACHING

the believer with power and energy for ministry service.[36] Charismatics believe that spiritual baptism is twofold. There is a pouring out of the Spirit at conversion and a second (subsequent) baptism of the Spirit for ministry empowerment. They preach that, first and foremost, the evidence of this second spiritual baptism is the manifestation of the gifts that the baptism bestows on believers. For most charismatics, proof of this event is "glossolalia," or speaking in tongues, which will be analyzed later in this chapter. Is the charismatics' interpretation of the Scriptures biblically sound from a theological perspective? Do charismatics present solid biblical evidence that corroborates their theological presupposition that formulates such teachings and preaching?

Charismatics Biblical Interpretation Argument

Charismatics argue that Scripture bears witness to a twofold experience.[37] The twofold experience interpreted by charismatics comes from the Synoptic Gospels, but some have ventured outside of the Gospels to justify this experience. Their interpretation of Matt 3:13–17, Mark 1:9–11, Luke 3:21–22, and John 1:32–33 focuses on Jesus' baptism, with the Holy Spirit first descending on him and leading him out into the wilderness for forty days to be tempted by Satan and then to return in the power of the Spirit. Charismatics assert that this is the second pouring out of the Spirit to empower Jesus for ministry, because he began doing miracles after that event.

Culpepper asserts that charismatics "point out that Jesus was born of the Holy Spirit (virgin birth) and was guided by the Holy Spirit throughout his infancy, youth, and young manhood ... before his ministry receiving an enduement with power from on high."[38] The charismatic interpretation of these passages in the four Gospels seems to point to Jesus first being born of the Holy Spirit, then

---

36. Culpepper, *Charismatic Movement*, 54.
37. Culpepper, *Charismatic Movement*, 56.
38. Culpepper, *Charismatic Movement*, 56.

being filled with the Spirit following baptism in water (a subsequent event), and then coming back from the wilderness in the power of the Spirit. Carismatics believe that if Jesus, the son of God, needed to be endowed with power for his ministry, then all who minister on his behalf need to be empowered by the Spirit as well.[39]

John F. MacArthur, a relevant advocate against charismatic dogma from a biblical perspective, relates:

> Most charismatics define Spirit baptism as a post-salvation, second blessing experience that adds something vital to what Christians receive at salvation. Spirit baptism, they believe, is usually accompanied by the evidence of speaking in tongues or perhaps other charismatic gifts. Such an experience is considered essential for any Christian who wants to know the fullness of divine and miraculous power in his or her life . . . but I am convinced that the fundamental teachings of the charismatic movement create an extreme emphasis on external evidences and thereby encourage bogus claims, false prophets, and other forms of spiritual humbug. Where such things flourish, there is bound to be a scandal—and the charismatic movement in the past decade has certainly been marked by more than the normal amount of scandal.[40]

John MacArthur provides strong arguments against the theological and biblical presuppositions of the charismatic movement, as well as the interpretations and dogma that formulate their doctrine, teaching, and preaching. However, MacArthur gives solace in the fact that many people in charismatic ministries preach Christ, and people come to him.[41] If charismatics are preaching Christ, then—as is the sole focus of this case study—can charismatic and expository preaching coexist as sound biblical doctrine for the edifying of the body of Christ? It has been established that both preaching methods must yield to the power and guidance of the Holy Spirit

---

39. Culpepper, *Charismatic Movement*, 57.
40. MacArthur, *Charismatic Chaos*, 20–21.
41. MacArthur, *Charismatic Chaos*, 21.

CHAPTER 2: EXPOSITORY AND CHARISMATIC PREACHING

and his anointing. As stated earlier, this provides common ground for the coexistence of both approaches.

Theological and biblical scholars agree in the academic sphere that charismatic doctrine has some merits theologically and biblically and has achieved great things for the body of Christ. However—concurring with MacArthur—although the charismatic movement is preaching Christ and souls are being converted, that should not exempt the charismatic movement or its teachings and preaching from careful biblical scrutiny.[42] As stewards of the word of God, Scripture admonishes us to "test them [prophecies] all; [to] hold on to what is good" (1 Thess 5:21).[43]

However, it is that experience that causes alarm in expository scholars. As MacArthur argues, "If charismatics are honest with themselves, [they] would have to acknowledge that personal experience—and not Scripture—is the foundation of their belief system . . . in their lives, the Scriptures too often rank second to experience."[44] First Corinthians 12-14 are the scriptures charismatics use to argue for their doctrine of spiritual gifts within the body of Christ.

MacArthur does not dismiss the charismatic experience, because experience has its place in the believer's life. It is the faith that induces this experience that confirms the belief that strengthens and empowers the believer in the sense of awe of God. It is one's faith that manifests the experience in the God that we serve. Therefore, experience has its place in developing disciples of Christ. MacArthur's argument is that "our faith should provide a basis for our experiences. An authentic spiritual experience will be the result of the quickening of truth in the Christian's mind—it does not occur in a mystical vacuum."[45]

Therefore, according to MacArthur, "Charismatics error because they tend to build their teachings on experience, rather than to understand that authentic experience happens in response

---

42. MacArthur, *Charismatic Chaos*, 22.
43. MacArthur, *Charismatic Chaos*, 22.
44. MacArthur, *Charismatic Chaos*, 23.
45. MacArthur, *Charismatic Chaos*, 23-24.

CHARISMATIC AND EXPOSITORY PREACHING

to the truth."[46] From MacArthur's perspective, if charismatics emphasize experience over biblical preaching and teaching, they are open to all kinds of false teachings, especially when it comes to spiritual gifts—these gifts cannot have precedence over God's word. Paul asserts in 1 Cor 12:4–11:

> There are different kinds of gifts, but the same Spirit distributes them. There are different kinds of service, but the same Lord. There are different kinds of working, but in all of them and in everyone it is the same God at work. Now to each one the manifestation of the Spirit is given for the common good. To one there is given through the Spirit a message of wisdom, to another a message of knowledge by means of the same Spirit, to another faith by the same Spirit, to another gifts of healing by that one Spirit, to another miraculous powers, to another prophecy, to another distinguishing between spirits, to another speaking in different kinds of tongues, and to still another the interpretation of tongues. All these are the work of one and the same Spirit, and he distributes them to each one, just as he determines.

Charismatics believe, like many other Christians in different denominations, that the spiritual gifts are there for the saints to utilize in the church in this modern era. Paul does not dismiss spiritual gifts to the believers in Corinth; he outlines how those gifts should be used within the church in an orderly fashion. Culpepper argues:

> The charismatic movement rightly emphasizes the body as the context for the operation of the gifts and the building up of the body for effective witness in the world as the purpose of their manifestation. Indeed one of the greatest contributions of the movement is the profound sense that expresses itself within it of Christians ministering to one another through the gifts that the Holy Spirit inspires.[47]

---

46. MacArthur, *Charismatic Chaos*, 24.
47. Culpepper, *Charismatic Movement*, 87.

CHAPTER 2: EXPOSITORY AND CHARISMATIC PREACHING

Expository and charismatic preachers all attest that spiritual gifts are present in the church and that every believer has a gift bestowed upon them by the Holy Spirit. Spiritual gifts are given for the body of Christ's edification and competence in spreading the gospel's good news to a dark world in need of the Savior (Jesus Christ). However, biblical theologians such as John MacArthur,[48] Jerry Vines and Jim Shaddix,[49] and Albert Mohler Jr.,[50] just to mention a few, view charismatic doctrine with cautious skepticism. Charismatics view spiritual gifts as spiritual power within the church to bring glory to God and his church.

As Culpepper points out, "Charismatics connect the operation of the gifts with spiritual power, often saying that as the character of Christ is demonstrated through the fruit of the Spirit (Galatians 5:22–23), so the power of Christ is manifested through the gifts (1 Corinthians 12:8–10)."[51] From Culpepper's point of view, there is a connection between the gifts and power; otherwise, they would have no value in edifying the body.[52]

Suppose charismatics view the spiritual gifts as spiritual power from a preaching perspective. What spiritual power is there in speaking in tongues if it is to edify the body of Christ? For many charismatics, speaking in tongues is the evidence of spiritual baptism. The believer is filled with the Spirit of God and can perform ministry duties empowered by the Holy Spirit. Many charismatic preachers, while in the middle of a sermon, digress and speak in tongues. They are captivating the congregation with utterances that they do not understand.

Nonetheless, the congregation embraces it, and many others begin to speak in utterances as well. How can speaking in tongues edify the body of Christ if what is said cannot be interpreted? Concerning this issue, we must examine it from a biblical perspective.

---

48. See MacArthur, *Charismatics* and *Charismatic Chaos*.
49. See Vines and Shaddix, *Power in the Pulpit*.
50. Mohler, "Charismatic Movement."
51. Culpepper, *Charismatic Movement*, 87.
52. Culpepper, *Charismatic Movement*, 87.

Glossolalia: "Speaking in Tongues"

New Hope Missionary Baptist Church, which has been my home church for over twenty years, was charismatic under the former pastor for about four years. During this time, the pastor introduced his charismatic doctrine, teaching that believers must be slain in the Spirit (spiritual baptism) to receive spiritual power, that the spiritual gifts would manifest themselves, and that as evidence of being filled with the Holy Ghost, one would begin to "speak in tongues." New Hope went from seven members to two hundred within a year, with most congregants speaking in tongues. It was amazing to see such rapid growth and people giving their lives to Christ. However, over time, it was apparent that over half of the members were there because of the pastor's charismatic gifts.

The anointing God had on the pastor's ministry overwhelmed him, and he started believing his "press clipping," thinking he was so divine and holy that he was above reproach and could do whatever he wanted in the church. Many charismatic preachers/pastors have fallen victim to losing sight of whom they serve and the power that belongs to God, thinking they generated such power from their ability. Many opponents of the charismatic movement view this as a dangerous, repetitious occurrence common within charismatic circles. Many charismatic preachers have been exposed and have fallen from grace. Servants of the Lord must always keep the Lord first in their ministry, be it charismatic or expository.

The preaching of this young charismatic preacher of New Hope had drawn many people to the small church. The worship services were filled with energy, which members viewed as the Holy Spirit's movement. However, people saw speaking in tongues as evidence of the church's spiritual power given by the Holy Spirit. Many charismatics view speaking in tongues as evidence of a spiritual baptism; however, is it biblically sound? The Bible does not command that all believers speak in tongues. However, there are commands to "be filled with the Spirit" (Eph 5:18) and to "walk by the Spirit" (Gal 5:16). First Corinthians 12:4–11 conveys to us that every believer has at least one spiritual gift and that some have the

CHAPTER 2: EXPOSITORY AND CHARISMATIC PREACHING

gift of tongues, but not all possess the gift of tongues. Therefore, why do charismatics preach and encourage members to speak in tongues? Culpepper notes:

> What biblical basis do charismatics have for interpreting tongues as a sign that one has received the baptism of the Spirit? Charismatics usually explain this along the following lines: When Paul asked the Ephesians, "Did you receive the Holy Spirit when you believed?" (Acts 19:2) He expected them to be able to answer very clearly one way or the other. For the early church, receiving the Holy Spirit was a very definite experience normally accompanied by charismatics manifestations, the most conspicuous of which was speaking in tongues. Speaking in tongues was one of the outward manifestations of the coming of the Holy Spirit at Pentecost (Acts 2).[53]

Theologians argue that this event at Pentecost, with the Holy Spirit coming on the apostles and speaking in foreign languages (tongues), was an event to establish the early church. However, does the gift of tongues apply to the contemporary church, as preached by many charismatic pastors? John MacArthur distinctively answers this question, stating:

> I am convinced by history, theology, and the Bible that tongues ceased in the apostolic age. And when it happened, they terminated altogether. The contemporary charismatic movement does not represent a revival of biblical tongues. It is an aberration similar to the practice of counterfeit tongues at Corinth. What evidence is there that tongues have ceased? First, tongues was a miraculous, revelatory gift, and as we have noted repeatedly, the age of miracles and revelation ended with the apostles. The last recorded miracles in the New Testament occurred around A.D. 58, with the healings on the island of Malta (Acts 28:7–10). From A.D. 58 to 96, when John finished the book of Revelation, no miracle is recorded.

---

53. Culpepper, *Charismatic Movement*, 90.

CHARISMATIC AND EXPOSITORY PREACHING

> Miracle gifts like tongues and healing are mentioned only in 1 Corinthians, an early epistle.[54]

Charismatic preachers, when closing the sermon with fervor, often speak in tongues and captivate the congregation. Believers join in with a symphony of utterances (speaking in tongues), jumping up and down, crying, and smiling. Their hearts seem to open for God to fill some void. People unfamiliar with charismatic worship would perceive this to be chaotic and scary. Nonetheless, people gravitate to this preaching, perceiving it by faith as a movement of the Holy Spirit simply because their experience was a movement of God in their lives.

One must ask whether the body of Christ was edified from this event. MacArthur asserts, "The gift of tongues was inferior to other gifts. It was given primarily as a sign (1 Cor 14:22) and cannot properly edify the church. It is also easily misused to edify self (1 Cor 14:4)."[55] MacArthur argues that the church gathers for the body's edification, not for self-gratification or personal experience seeking.[56] From this perspective, tongues had limited usefulness in the church and was never intended as a permanent gift.[57] Paul states in 1 Cor 14:1–5:

> Follow the way of love and eagerly desire gifts of the Spirit, especially prophecy. For anyone who speaks in a tongue does not speak to people but to God. Indeed, no one understands them; they utter mysteries by the Spirit. But the one who prophesies speaks to people for their strengthening, encouraging and comfort. Anyone who speaks in a tongue edifies themselves, but the one who prophesies edifies the church. I would like every one of you to speak in tongues, but I would rather have you prophesy. The one who prophesies is greater than the

---

54. MacArthur, *Charismatic Chaos*, 231.

55. MacArthur, *Charismatic Chaos*, 232. See also MacArthur, *Ashamed of the Gospel*.

56. MacArthur, *Charismatic Chaos*, 232.

57. MacArthur, *Charismatic Chaos*, 232.

CHAPTER 2: EXPOSITORY AND CHARISMATIC PREACHING

one who speaks in tongues, unless someone interprets, so that the church may be edified.

Most advocates against charismatic doctrine and preaching view speaking in tongues as neither miraculous (as many charismatics claim) nor as a pathological or diabolical phenomenon (as many of its critics may argue).[58] Poloma describes speaking in tongues as "a form of non-discursive prayer, a pre-conceptual expression of spontaneous prayer. To the uninitiated, it appears as babbling in nonsense syllables and involves altered states of consciousness. To the believer, it is a surrendering of mind and heart to a form of prayer believed to be biblically encouraged."[59] Charismatic preaching with the manifestation of spiritual gifts by all accounts resonates with Christian believers. Although some may not acknowledge it openly, they desire the spiritual gifts that bring awe of God into their lives, the same gifts that the apostles displayed in the early church, where God's power and his Spirit advanced the Christian movement. Those at Pentecost heard the word with the Holy Spirit's power on display, empowering the apostles with spiritual gifts, and they believed and gave themselves over to Christ and the apostles' teachings.

In most charismatic worship services, the Holy Spirit's gifts are manifested and captivate the congregation. By the Holy Spirit's unction, Charismatic preachers preach so tantalizingly that people flock to the services by the hundreds. In many of the services, the manifestation of the Spirit's gifts is on display, like speaking in tongues, the laying on of hands, and prophesying. However, as Poloma notes, "Of all of the gifts of the Holy Spirit, glossolalia has most fascinated secular researchers and non-Pentecostal theologians and has provided subject matter for charismatics."[60] Critics of the charismatic movement concede that it has made a tremendous impact on Christianity. Poloma asserts:

---

58. Poloma, *Charismatic Movement*, 52.
59. Poloma, *Charismatic Movement*, 52.
60. Poloma, *Charismatic Movement*, 52.

CHARISMATIC AND EXPOSITORY PREACHING

Charismatics have demonstrated the need that people have to participate actively in worship and have shown other Christians the need for greater commitment. Thus, even some unsympathetic critics of charismatic theology have come to recognize its religious impact. Charismatic teachings often warn against overemphasizing religious experience and are critical of those who skip from group to group in search of new religious experience or new "highs." The emphasis, most will say, must remain on the giver and not on his gifts. If the experience is from God, it is meant to bear fruit; it is meant to be a source of loving service to others. The psychologist-priest John Powell (1974, pp. 54–55) has argued that a genuine religious experience must be lasting, have a real effect on the believer, and be directed toward the spiritual enrichment of others. Taken as a whole, the charismatic movement seems to meet these criteria.[61]

Critics of the charismatic movement attest to some merits the movement possesses concerning Christian dogma which benefit the church and advance the gospel, leading people to Christ. There are positive aspects of charismatic theology and preaching; even expository preachers have adopted some charismatic preaching methods by invoking the Holy Spirit's movement and gifts. The research goal is to bridge that gap between expository and charismatic preaching to find common ground from a hermeneutical foundation, combining the two homiletically.

Therefore, charismatic doctrine must be evaluated extensively to understand the arguments for and against its theology and interpretation of Scriptures. For this research, both preaching methods (expository and charismatic) must be harmonized from an exegetical perspective regarding Scripture, since the different interpretations of Scripture are what divides the two. Although biblical scholars view expository preaching as the bedrock of homiletics, charismatic preaching cannot be ignored, because it has contributed a great deal to the gospel's advancement, and souls are being saved, accepting Christ as their Savior.

61. Poloma, *Charismatic Movement*, 82.

CHAPTER 2: EXPOSITORY AND CHARISMATIC PREACHING

Arguments against Charismatic Exegesis (Interpretation)

John MacArthur staunchly points to four texts that he believes charismatics repeatedly misinterpret: Matt 12:22–31, Heb 13:8, Mark 16:17-18, and 1 Pet 2:24. First, MacArthur asserts that charismatics misinterpret Matt 12:22–31 in defense of their usage of spiritual gifts, such as speaking in tongues and the laying on of hands for healing or any action that the charismatic movement would consider an act of the Holy Spirit—which, if anyone refutes it, would come perilously close to that person committing the unpardonable sin of blasphemy against the Holy Spirit.[62]

The second contention regards Heb 13:8, which charismatics use as a proof text to confirm that Jesus is the same yesterday and today and forever.[63] Charismatics interpret this passage of Scripture to mean that the works Jesus did in his earthly ministry apply to Christians today, who possess the same spiritual power to continue doing the works of Christ for the upbuilding of the kingdom. MacArthur's question is this: "Does the Pentecostal and charismatic interpretation of Hebrews 13:8 stand up to inspection according to sound hermeneutical principles?"[64] The literal meaning of the verse is plain. Jesus Christ is unchanging yesterday, today, and forever. MacArthur proceeds to explain, "When tested by sound hermeneutical principles, the charismatic interpretation of Hebrews 13:8 does not stand up. Charismatics force into the verse a meaning that is not there in order to justify their contention that tongues, miracles, and healings are happening today just as they did in the first century."[65]

Third, MacArthur insists that Mark 16:17–18 is a misinterpretation of Scripture by charismatics who claim that this passage means that believers in Christ walk in spiritual power and are protected from all dangers, seen or unseen. To provide a Pentecostal

---

62. MacArthur, *Charismatic Chaos*, 97.
63. MacArthur, *Charismatic Chaos*, 99.
64. MacArthur, *Charismatic Chaos*, 99.
65. MacArthur, *Charismatic Chaos*, 100.

CHARISMATIC AND EXPOSITORY PREACHING

perspective, MacArthur cites Oscar Vouga's usage of the passage when he (MacArthur) states, "Through faith in the name of Jesus, devils are being cast out today, and many are being delivered from powers of darkness, into the kingdom of God. Signs are following the preaching of the gospel where it is preached in faith, and with the anointing of the Holy Spirit and power."[66] MacArthur's criticism is derived from the preacher's lack of addressing the entire text in his interpretation of the passage. From MacArthur's perspective, this is the same kind of understanding theological liberals use to twist Bible passages to fit what they want them to mean.[67]

Finally, 1 Pet 2:24 is another passage that MacArthur argues that charismatics misinterpret to defend their doctrine on the gift of healing. MacArthur's biblical insight on Scripture exposes many flaws in the hermeneutical process of charismatics. He points out that charismatics interpret this passage to mean that Christ's death provides physical healing to those who are in Christ.[68] However, sound exegesis reveals that Christ's death was to heal the sickness of sin in humanity. The expository approach reveals the truth that the healing of sin was the reason why Christ suffered, was mortally wounded, died, and gave up his spirit (1 Pet 2:24) for humanity's salvation.

Preaching the word of God comes with tremendous responsibility, and interpretation is at the center of rightly conveying the word (2 Tim 2:15). F. B. Meyer notes from an expository viewpoint:

> Our Lord was careful to consider the text in relation to the context and the whole tenor and teaching of Scripture. The habit of taking a little snippet of a verse from any part of the Bible and making it the subject of discourse exposes the preacher to the danger of an unbalanced statement of truth, which is very prejudicial. Nothing is more perilous than the partial knowledge of

---

66. MacArthur, *Charismatic Chaos*, 100.
67. MacArthur, *Charismatic Chaos*, 101.
68. MacArthur, *Charismatic Chaos*, 124.

CHAPTER 2: EXPOSITORY AND CHARISMATIC PREACHING

God's truth, which is based on sentences torn from their rock-bed and viewed in isolation from their setting.[69]

Interpretation of specific passages in the Bible is what divides expository and charismatic preaching. Considering Heb 13:8, charismatics preach that Jesus is unchanging, that the works he did during his earthly ministry are manifested today in the church, or at least available for the church to utilize. Critics may disagree with this interpretation, but some expository preachers preach this from their pulpits as well. Like charismatics, they assert that there are spiritual gifts in the church and that Jesus/God is unchanging. These gifts may not be used to the same extent as when the apostles established the church, but these gifts remain today. Claiming that the Spirit's gifts are no longer active in the church alludes to the absence of the Holy Spirit's power, which is part of the Godhead. The Holy Spirit empowers charismatic and expository preaching; without the Holy Spirit, there is no spiritual power. Though theologians and biblical scholars may find flaws in charismatic doctrine and interpretations, common ground can be found between the two preaching methods. There is a state of parallelism regarding the two preaching methods because it is the same Spirit that dwells and empowers the two. Still, opponents against the charismatic interpretations of Scripture (exegesis) provide valid arguments that, if overlooked, would jeopardize the inerrancy and authority of God's word.

Therefore, both charismatics and expository preachers share a commonality in interpreting God's word from a hermeneutical approach. William W. Klein, Craig L. Blomberg, and Robert L. Hubbard Jr., in their book *Introduction to Biblical Interpretation*, explain:

> Hermeneutics is essential for a valid interpretation of the Bible. Instead of piously insisting that we will simply allow God to speak to us from his Word, we contend that to ensure we hear God's voice rather than our culture's voice or our own biases, we need to interpret the Scriptures in a systematic and careful fashion. We need . . . proper

69. Meyer, *Expository Preaching*, 78.

hermeneutics. If we are to understand God's truth for ourselves (and to teach or preach it to others), we must discover precisely what God intended to communicate. A careful system of hermeneutics provides the means for the interpreter to arrive at the text's intention to understand what God intended to communicate through human minds and hands. A careful approach to hermeneutics provides the means for the interpreter to arrive at what God intended to communicate. Some conservative Christians abuse the Bible by their proof-texting. They use the Bible like a telephone book of texts they cite by chapter and verse to prove their viewpoint. This can lead to many distortions and errors that could be avoided by using hermeneutics. Hermeneutics safeguards the Scriptures against misuse by people who, deliberately or not, distort the Bible for their own ends. Proper hermeneutics provides the conceptual framework for interpreting correctly by means of accurate exegesis. Exegesis puts into practice one's theory of interpretation. Thus proper hermeneutics will generate proper exegetical methods.[70]

Hermeneutics is essential to interpreting God's word for application for the contemporary church. Critics such as John MacArthur, Jerry Vines, and Chris Hand are vindicated, because their research reveals flaws in charismatic doctrine and scriptural interpretation. However, as formerly stated, they also assert that the charismatic movement's positive aspects have contributed to Christianity's advancement. Chris Hand, commenting on MacArthur's perspective, notes, "From MacArthur's perspective, desperate times call for desperate measures. They can agree to disagree about tongues and prophecy because other items on which they agree—such as reformed soteriology[,] complementary gender roles, and church disciplines[—]demand more urgent attention."[71]

There is common ground for charismatic and expository preaching, although there is a dispute regarding hermeneutical issues that can be solved by putting specific passages in a proper

---

70. Klein et al., *Biblical Interpretation*, 19–20.
71. Hand, "Charismatic Movement," 13.

CHAPTER 2: EXPOSITORY AND CHARISMATIC PREACHING

context. Charismatic interpretation of the spiritual gifts is a subject on which both methods can find common ground, because neither approach is helpful if the Holy Spirit does not empower it; the same Spirit empowers the entire church.

The Holy Spirit Validates Both Preaching Methods

The Holy Spirit must validate charismatic and expository preaching. The Holy Spirit bears witness to and empowers what is done in the body of Christ; nothing is done without the help of the Holy Spirit. Christ promised that the Holy Spirit "will guide you into all the truth. He will not speak on his own; he will speak only what he hears, and he will tell you what is yet to come. He will glorify me because it is from me that he will receive what he will make known to you" (John 16:13-14). Charismatic and expository preaching methods have charism as a ministry.

Webster defines charism, also pronounced "charisma," in the following way: "The power or quality of winning the devotion of large numbers of people or great personal magnetism; Charm or a divinely inspired gift or power, as the ability to perform miracles."[72]

From this perspective, charismatic and expository preaching are on familiar ground. Therefore, examining case studies on these two preaching methods is essential to the church's mission: reaching the lost, spreading the gospel's good news, revealing Christ to a dark world in need of this marvelous light that shines through the darkness. The Holy Spirit is the one who makes both charismatic and expository preaching relevant. Regarding charism, Kilian McDonnell conveys, "In the New Testament *charism* are operations or manifestations of the Holy Spirit in and for the Christian community. 'To each is given the manifestation of the Spirit for the common good' (1 Cor 12:7)."[73] McDonnell also notes, "A person may seek the charisms (1 Cor 12:31), but they are essentially spirit gifts. The gifts are without number, as

---

72. *Webster's II New Riverside University Dictionary* (1984), s.v. "charisma."
73. McDonnell, *Charismatic Renewal*, 6.

they are the multitudinous ways that the Holy Spirit comes to visibility in the church in service functions. To a greater or lesser degree, a charism is a ministry to others."[74]

Although charismatic and expository preachers have the same Spirit that empowers, it is the doctrine that divides the two when invoking the Holy Spirit's help in the ministry of preaching. However, Culpepper points out the following concerning the charismatic position on their doctrine: "Most leaders of the charismatic movement claim to ground such doctrinal views, not on their experience, but on the teachings of Holy Scripture. They insist that in all cases, Scripture provides the norm."[75]

He proceeds to explain, "Charismatics believe that the interpretation of Scripture should not be weakened in order to conform to contemporary experience; rather, contemporary Christian experience should be blessed and empowered until it conforms to the pattern of Scripture."[76] If this is true from a charismatic perspective, they have more in common with expository preaching than they realize. Heisler notes, "The Spirit of God and the Word of God are not antagonistic, and any attempt to put them at odds is unbiblical and theologically irresponsible . . . the Word of God and the Spirit of God are in constant, continuous, and complementary relationship to each other."[77]

Therefore, it is essential to research these two preaching methods, considering the tremendous influence and growth charismatics are experiencing in their churches. If these preaching methods can be integrated, the body of Christ can be more effective in spreading the gospel, especially at the local-church level. The number of people that would give their lives to Christ just by hearing the word preached from these two methods—which can only enhance spreading the gospel—would be astronomical. The charismatic movement has experienced tremendous success in ministry. So,

---

74. McDonnell, *Charismatic Renewal*, 6.
75. Culpepper, *Charismatic Movement*, 53.
76. Culpepper, *Charismatic Movement*, 53.
77. Heisler, *Spirit-Led Preaching*, 62.

CHAPTER 2: EXPOSITORY AND CHARISMATIC PREACHING

from a Christian perspective, is this a genuine move, or manifestation, of the Holy Spirit in this contemporary church age? The Holy Spirit's presence must be experienced and manifested in the lives of believers. People of God need that boost from the Spirit at times to know that God is there. The manifestation of spiritual gifts provides that awe of God. The works of the Holy Spirit must be active in the church. Charismatics and expository preachers stand on this belief. Charismatics are not the only ones who advocate this. Many expository believers agree that the Holy Spirit must be active in church life.

Those who stand firm on expository preaching principles contend that expository preaching is the first vehicle of advancing the word with truth and correctness. However, the Holy Spirit must be the guide that strengthens all preaching. Expository and charismatics both submit to *Sola scriptura*, the principle that God's word is the only basis for divine authority.[78] Critics such as MacArthur fear that the influence of charismatic teachings may cause many in the church to abandon its cornerstone, which is the word of God—the divine authority of Christian dogma—and gravitate more to spiritual experience.[79] Many biblical scholars may share MacArthur's sentiments as well, but what cannot be ignored are the conversions of the many people who receive and respond to the preaching and ministry of charismatics.

The Holy Spirit will only work on God's behalf, manifesting the truths of Christ and empowering the church to do God's will. There is another reality: Satan is the master at work to hinder Christ's work. The church must guard against false doctrines that have a sense of godliness, as it is the enemy's work to lead God's people astray. Therefore, it is incumbent on believers to always walk in the Spirit, for it is the Spirit that provides discernment regarding those things that are not of Christ. Gordon D. Fee notes that "the role of the Spirit is on earth, indwelling believers in

---

78. MacArthur, *Charismatic Chaos*, 56.
79. MacArthur, *Charismatic Chaos*, 56.

order to help them in the weakness of their present existence and thereby to intercede on their behalf."[80]

Conclusion

Chapter 2 explored the differences between the charismatic and expository preaching methods. In this chapter, charismatic doctrine was examined, because it is the doctrine that formulates the preaching method of charismatic preachers. It was necessary to view its significance, considering that expository preaching is the bedrock of sound biblical preaching for most biblical scholars.

Throughout this chapter, for research purposes, viewing the history of the charismatic movement, its interpretations of Scripture, and its theological views was essential to understanding the issues that divide charismatic and expository preachers. The purpose of conducting this case study of these preaching methods is to determine if both ways can be integrated into one sound doctrine for the benefit of the church.

The research revealed that charismatic doctrine has some flaws in its interpretation of specific passages from Scripture. Although expository preaching is grounded in a hermeneutical approach, charismatics are held to this same method of study of the word of God. Charismatics and expository preachers are empowered by the same Spirit that empowers Christ's church; therefore, common ground is established between the two. Despite the minor issues being debated, achieving unity is possible, because the arguments are valid and mitigated.

The mitigating factor is that the Spirit of God and the word of God are empowering both preaching methods. They complement each other from a Spirit-filled preaching perspective, because together, word and Spirit work in powerful unity that establishes the theological foundation for Spirit-filled preaching.[81] Charismatic and expository preachers must partake in the

80. Fee, *God's Empowering Presence*, 838.
81. Heisler, *Spirit-Led Preaching*, 62.

CHAPTER 2: EXPOSITORY AND CHARISMATIC PREACHING

rigorous work of hermeneutics to understand the original intent and truth of God's word to present to his people. Word and Spirit are the catalysts to all sound preaching, because, according to Heisler, "the Word activates the Spirit, and the Spirit authenticates the Word. The Word is the instrument of the Spirit, and the Spirit is the implement of the Word. The Word is the written witness, and the Spirit is the inward witness."[82]

Therefore, the word is the source and substance of preaching, the Spirit is the supernatural power in preaching, and charismatics and expository preachers must stand firm on these principles to maintain sound preaching doctrine.[83] Charismatics are correct in their assertion that the Holy Spirit is at work in the church and active in believers' lives. Expository preachers confirm the assertion that the Holy Spirit is involved in all aspects of the church. However, charismatics proclaim that speaking in tongues is confirmation of being filled with the Spirit.

When charismatics make such a proclamation, they are putting the gift of tongues above all other gifts as proof of the indwelling of the Spirit in one's life. However, when charismatics assert that speaking in tongues is the ultimate evidence of being filled with the Spirit, they are in error. In his letter to the believers in Corinth, Paul, for this very reason, puts into perspective the gifts of the Spirit (1 Cor 12).

Paul wanted the believers in Corinth to know that there are many gifts of the Spirit, and that every believer in Christ has been given some spiritual gift for the edifying of the body of Christ (1 Cor 12:4–11). The issue of speaking in tongues creates a theological argument from an expository perspective because of Paul's view of the Spirit's gifts. Paul acknowledges that speaking in tongues does not edify the body of Christ and only edifies the individual (1 Cor 14:1–5). Charismatics interpret Acts 2:4 ("All of them were filled with the Holy Spirit and began to speak in other tongues as the Spirit enabled them") to mean that believers must possess the gift of tongues as evidence of the Spirit

---

82. Heisler, *Spirit-Led Preaching*, 62.
83. Heisler, *Spirit-Led Preaching*, 62.

dwelling within them. However, a careful hermeneutical study of that same passage reveals that this occurrence was for the formation of Christ's church; the gift of tongues is there for the church's usage. When the Holy Spirit came upon the disciples on the day of Pentecost, they received spiritual power and gifts, first manifested as speaking in tongues; this gift was necessary for the establishment of Christ's church, because there were God-fearing Jews from every nation on earth and Gentiles that spoke different languages present during this event.

Therefore, the gift of tongues was given so that the apostles could speak to all in their language (Acts 2:4–41)—so that all would hear the gospel of a new age through Christ Jesus and the sacrifice he made on the cross for the penalty of humanity's sins in order to be reconciled back to God, first the Jew and then the Gentile. The gift of tongues is still available to believers, but used in different capacities.

The Holy Spirit bestows these gifts according to God's will to be used for his purpose. Speaking in tongues does not in itself confirm the indwelling of God's Spirit; it is the love that individuals display toward one another and to the world—Christ's love that was illuminated on the cross—that confirms the Spirit's indwelling power in believers. If charismatics hold to this gift as confirmation of the Spirit's indwelling, one could easily be deceived. It is incumbent on ministers of the gospel, whether charismatic or expository, to understand that the essential role of the Holy Spirit in the life of the church is cooperating with Jesus in the exegesis of Scripture.[84] The issue of speaking in tongues as being evidence of the indwelling of the Holy Spirit in a believer's life is one of the major issues that divide charismatic and expository preachers in their biblical interpretation of Scripture.

---

84. Vondey, *Holy Spirit*, 110.

Chapter 3: Issues That Divide Charismatic and Expository Preaching

Throughout the academic world, biblical and theological scholars debate the hermeneutical position of the charismatic movement's doctrine, which is the foundation of its preaching and ministry. At the center of the debate is the Holy Spirit's work and the spiritual gifts bestowed upon believers in their spiritual walk, which biblical scholars and theologians alike view as a "pneumatology" (doctrine of the Holy Spirit) issue. Advocates against charismatic doctrine and preaching reveal that charismatics are in error regarding their interpretation of Scripture concerning the Holy Spirit's divine function at believers' conversion, as well as their belief that the distribution of spiritual gifts is evidence of a "subsequential event" of the "baptism of the Holy Spirit."

Charismatics assert that "Spirit baptism," which they view as the believer's baptism, is the filling of the believer with the Holy Spirit's power and presence for ministry. They also assert that the confirmation of this event in the believers' life is glossolalia, or speaking in tongues. Despite some theological differences in the relationship between glossolalia and the Spirit's baptism, many charismatic Christians date their baptism of the Spirit to the first time they spoke in tongues.[1]

Margaret Poloma explains, "Most Pentecostals emphasize that glossolalia is the definitive evidence of Spirit baptism, while neo-Pentecostals are more likely to assert that glossolalia is only

---

1. Poloma, *Charismatic Movement*, 70.

CHARISMATIC AND EXPOSITORY PREACHING

one indication."[2] According to Poloma, "Those who accept classical Pentecostal teachings will recount their first experience with glossolalia when asked about Spirit baptism, but neo-Pentecostal testimonies (even from those who pray in tongues) may or may not include such a reference."[3] In other words, from a neo-Pentecostal's perspective, different spiritual gifts other than glossolalia (speaking in tongues) may confirm the same spiritual baptism.

There must be a formulated approach to conveying God's word to his people. First, understanding the ideology of charismatic and expository preaching methods must be explored. For most biblical scholars, expository preaching is the foundation for conveying God's word to humanity, the saved and unsaved alike. Biblical expositors are preachers who hold to the unadulterated word of God. According to Scripture, they preach only God's truth, not adding or taking away from what Scripture conveys to its audience—the author's primary intent. Therefore, speaking in tongues has little effect in the preaching methods of charismatic and expository preachers, simply because if there is no one to interpret what is said, then the congregants cannot be edified by what is said in a different language.

This method of preaching is a formulation of hermeneutics. Hermeneutics, as explained by William W. Klein, Craig L. Blomberg, and Robert L. Hubbard Jr., "describes the task of explaining the meaning of the Scriptures . . . it describes the principles people use to understand what something means, to comprehend what a message [that] is written, oral, or visual is endeavoring to communicate."[4]

However, this does not resolve the issue that divides charismatic and expository preaching, because charismatic and expository preachers both must partake in the oasis of hermeneutical endeavors to correctly convey God's word to his people. Therefore, the purpose of chapter 3 is to provide research methods from an intervention approach that will help resolve or bring

2. Poloma, *Charismatic Movement*, 72.
3. Poloma, *Charismatic Movement*, 72
4. Klein et al., *Biblical Interpretation*, 4.

CHAPTER 3: ISSUES THAT DIVIDE

clarity to the issues surrounding expository and charismatic preaching regarding their preaching approach to Scripture from a theological and doctrinal perspective.

I hypothesize that charismatic and expository preaching can be integrated with the correct application of Scriptures through the process of exegesis, hermeneutics, and homiletics to be even more effective in preaching. Therefore, this research's methodology is the intervention approach, a form of qualitative research that provides an abundance of techniques to evaluate this theory.

The intervention approach will be in the form of a case study of these two preaching methods that involves visiting three churches that have charismatic and expository preaching styles to observe these preaching methods in action. The case study's focus will be on both preaching methods' effectiveness on the congregants, worship service, ministry, and church growth. This research method helps in congregational and parachurch settings, because it helps a diverse group of participants become more aware of their church's issues.[5]

Purpose and Objectives of the Research's Intervention

I will observe both preaching methods and evaluate their effectiveness, the congregants' response to the church's preached message, and its growth by visiting three churches for this case study. The objective is to compare these preaching styles to determine if there is a correlation that would support this research hypothesis: that charismatic and expository preaching can coexist as a profound doctrine preached for the body of Christ's edification. Also, within the scope of this intervention process, all pastors and deacon chairpersons will be interviewed concerning their theological position and preaching methods.

Three members from each church congregation will complete a questionnaire. The time limit for the interviews and

5. Sensing, *Qualitative Research*, 141.

completion of questionnaires will be approximately thirty minutes for each participant. However, the evaluation of the intervention is a crucial component of the research project.[6] It allows me to obtain data to mitigate the issues that divide charismatic and expository preaching methods.

People Involved: Purposive Sampling

The people involved in this research are the pastors, deacon chairpersons, and three members from each church congregation. Each pastor will select three members and obtain their consent to participate in the study, although they will be anonymous to me. Each member chosen should be knowledgeable of their church functions and doctrine to answer the questionnaire concisely. The purposive sampling is designed to select people who are aware of their church doctrine and the order of their worship service, which are the essentials needed for this research. Therefore, the information received from all participants and the analysis of the church worship service and preaching will serve to address the issues concerning the two preaching methods.[7]

By observing the worship service and taking notes of each preacher's charismatic or expository delivery style, interpretation of Scripture, doctrine, and the response from the congregation, valuable information will be gathered for me to evaluate both preaching methods and the effects on the church. Most importantly, assessing the pastors' theological positions on scriptures conveyed and preached to the congregation on those Sundays will help formulate a strategy to implement both preaching methods as a combined preaching style.

In preparation for preaching a sermon, every preacher, be they charismatic or expository, must begin with these four principles in mind: (1) exegesis, (2) hermeneutics, (3) homiletics, and (4) exposition. Jerry Vines and Jim Shaddix assert how such principles are

---

6. Sensing, *Qualitative Research*, 79.
7. Sensing, *Qualitative Research*, 83.

CHAPTER 3: ISSUES THAT DIVIDE

essential when they state, "The very nature of preaching demands that the preacher applies the process of exposition. Viewing this process as a journey can help on this road to communicate God's revelation rightly."[8] Therefore, observing the preached word from these pastors will be crucial to the research.

Defining these key terms ("exegesis," "hermeneutics," "homiletics," and "exposition") in the process of preaching is vital to understanding charismatic and expository preaching. Therefore, Jerry Vines and Jim Shaddix define these key terms in such a profound way when they state:

> The road to exposition begins with careful exegesis. This can be defined as the procedure one follows for discovering the Holy Spirit's intent in a Bible passage . . . hermeneutics, the science of interpreting what a passage of Scripture means . . . homiletics, the art, and science of saying the same thing that the text of Scripture says. Technically, it is the study of sermon preparation. When delivery is added to this whole process of exegesis, hermeneutics, and homiletics, the result can be described as exposition, which means to lay open.[9]

Observing both preaching methods is critical to this research; however, specific Scripture passages—discussed in the previous chapters—on which charismatics base their theology and doctrine must be examined to formulate a strategy to combine both preaching styles.

Therefore, to combine both preaching styles, an exegetical and hermeneutical study will be performed on 1 Cor 12–14, which concerns spiritual gifts, and other passages (which will be revealed later) on the Holy Spirit's function in the believer's life from a charismatic and expository interpretation. Preben Vang provides theological insight concerning these issues by stating, "Spiritual gifts are communal and not given for mere personal benefit. God grants the gifts of his Spirit to enable the Christ community to manifest Christ and to continue his ministry of revealing the

---

8. Vines and Shaddix, *Power in the Pulpit*, 27.
9. Vines and Shaddix, *Power in the Pulpit*, 27–28.

presence of God's kingdom (Mk 1:15)."[10] The theological insight is that the gifts of the Spirit about which charismatics preach and teach were given to manifest God's power to unbelievers at an appointed time, and even to the household of faith when their faith is lacking. The Holy Spirit's power should not be quenched, because these gifts should not only be displayed in charismatic-based churches but in the universal church as a whole.

The task is to find common ground biblically to substantiate my hypothesis that charismatic interpretations of the Scripture passages concerning spiritual gifts and the Holy Spirit's movement in believers' lives are not that distant from expository interpretations. While I have found slight errors in some charismatic interpretations, I argue that such errors are due to the eisegesis that marks their approach to specific Scripture passages.

Biblical Task

The biblical task consists of reexamining charismatic interpretations of 1 Cor 12–14; Matt 12:22–31; John 16:7–11; Mark 16:17–18; Acts 1:5–8; 2:3; 2:4; 4:31; Rom 15:19; 1 Cor 2:4; and Gal 3:5. These passages were chosen because they constitute some of the key scriptures charismatics use as the foundation of their theology and doctrine. Examining these scriptures from a charismatic and expository perspective will greatly contribute to a solution concerning the issues that divide these two preaching methods.

Theologians such as John F. MacArthur, Jerry Vines, and Jim Shaddix believe that the charismatics' profound error is their interpretation of the Holy Spirit's empowerment of believers at conversion and subsequential empowerment for ministry after the transformation into the body of Christ. MacArthur argues that charismatic dogma all starts with the baptism of the Spirit.[11] MacArthur asserts, "Charismatics generally believe that after someone becomes a Christian, he or she must seek diligently for

---

10. Vang, *1 Corinthians*, 169.
11. MacArthur, *Charismatic Chaos*, 26.

CHAPTER 3: ISSUES THAT DIVIDE

the baptism in the Spirit. Those who get this baptism also experience various phenomena, such as speaking in tongues, feelings of euphoria, visions, and emotional outbursts."[12]

The experience of being baptized in the Spirit is the foundation upon which much of the charismatic belief system stands.[13] Charismatics' support of this belief system starts with their interpretation of the book of Acts. In Acts 1:5-8, where Jesus is talking with his disciples before his ascension concerning the Holy Spirit, he states:

> "For John baptized with water, but in a few days you will be baptized with the Holy Spirit."
>
> Then they gathered around him and asked him, "Lord, are you at this time going to restore the kingdom to Israel?"
>
> He said to them: "It is not for you to know the times or dates the Father has set by his own authority. But you will receive power when the Holy Spirit comes on you; and you will be my witnesses in Jerusalem, and in all Judea and Samaria, and to the ends of the earth."

Charismatic preaching and interpretation of this passage declares that when a person receives Christ and is baptized, that individual should receive the Holy Spirit's power for service. However, charismatics assert that empowerment occurs later, when that individual receives a *baptism of the Spirit* and only then is empowered for service (which they view as a subsequential event). Expository interpretation argues that charismatics are in error with their understanding of a subsequent event. From an expository position, when people come to Christ and are baptized, the Holy Spirit is upon them even before baptism. The Holy Spirit convicted the believer's heart in the first place and dwells with them throughout the conversion process and beyond, leading and empowering the believer for service.

Charismatics and expository preachers concur in that all Christians should be walking in the power of the Holy Spirit and

---

12. MacArthur, *Charismatic Chaos*, 26.
13. MacArthur, *Charismatic Chaos*, 171.

that it is the Holy Spirit who imparts spiritual gifts to believers. Expository theologians such as Robert Culpepper argue that beginning with the Holy Spirit's arrival at Pentecost, instituting a new order—from then on—the Holy Spirit comes at the moment of faith and indwells the believer in a permanent, abiding relationship. Culpepper explains:

> Most Protestant Neo-Pentecostals follow Pentecostalism in distinguishing baptism in the Spirit from conversion. This baptism does not relate to an experience of salvation but is one in which the Christian is empowered for ministry in Christ's name. In conversion, the Holy Spirit comes to dwell in the believer (Roman[s] 8:9), and through his indwelling presence, life is imparted. Through the baptism in the Spirit, there is a release of the Spirit so that rivers of living water flow out from the believer (John 7:37–38).[14]

Charismatics view the movement of the Holy Spirit through different lenses, with an emphasis on experience. Their interpretation is twofold. First, an individual is baptized with water following conversion. Second, they receive the baptism of the Spirit. When an individual is baptized by total immersion in water, this is an outward expression of accepting Christ as their Lord and Savior (conversion), and the Holy Spirit is imparted at that time; however, charismatics contend that this is not related to the baptism of the Spirit. Acts 2:3–4, from the charismatic's perspective, is the core supportive passage concerning their claims about the Holy Spirit's baptism. In Acts 2:3–4, Luke says, "They saw what seemed to be tongues of fire that separated and came to rest on each of them. All of them were filled with the Holy Spirit and began to speak in other tongues as the Spirit enabled them." Concerning charismatic theology and interpretation of Acts 2:3–4, MacArthur states:

> The second chapter of Acts is the key passage of Scripture from which Pentecostals and charismatics develop their theology of the baptism of the Holy Spirit. Pentecostals [sic] and charismatic doctrine of subsequence

14. Culpepper, *Charismatic Movement*, 54–55.

CHAPTER 3: ISSUES THAT DIVIDE

are drawn primarily from that passage. Charismatics point out that the apostles and other disciples who experienced the baptism tongues in Acts 2:1-4 had already been saved. Here at Pentecost, they were receiving the power of the Holy Spirit, which they would use to change the world. On those points, the charismatic view cannot be faulted. We can be confident that the disciples mentioned in Acts 2, at least some of them had experienced salvation . . . how do we know that some of them were already saved? Jesus had told His apostles, "Rejoice that your names are recorded in heaven" (Luke 10:20), and "You are already clean because of the word which I have spoken" (John 15:3). There is no doubt that he was affirming their salvation.[15]

Charismatics' interpretation of John 20:21-22 is ambiguous, because Jesus did, in fact, state to the disciples, "Receive the Holy Spirit," in the upper room after his resurrection in verse 22, but later passages do not confirm this receiving of the Spirit in John 20:21-22. MacArthur asserts that charismatics suggest that Jesus' disciples had already received the Holy Spirit before Pentecost—that is, after the resurrection in the upper room when Jesus appeared to them and breathed on them, according to John 20:21-22. However, the experience of the Holy Spirit on the day of Pentecost was, in fact, a permanent indwelling of the Holy Spirit that gave them the power for service in carrying out the Great Commission.[16]

MacArthur refutes this charismatic interpretation of John 20:21-22 from an expository perspective. MacArthur suggests that the disciples did not receive the Holy Spirit at the time when Jesus breathed on them and said, "Receive the Holy Spirit" (John 20:22), because they did not walk in spiritual power or manifest any spiritual power until the Holy Spirit came upon all of them on the day of Pentecost.[17] John 20:22, for the most part, is an

---

15. MacArthur, *Charismatic Chaos*, 175-76.
16. MacArthur, *Charismatic Chaos*, 175-76.
17. MacArthur, *Charismatic Chaos*, 176.

ambiguous passage of Scripture from the perspective of charismatic and expository interpretation.

This passage could guide charismatic and expository preaching into eisegesis if concise semantic study is neglected. Therefore, in that context, what did Jesus mean when he said to the disciples, "Receive the Holy Spirit" (John 20:22)? Advocates of the interpretive (expository) approach and methods refute the way charismatics interpret this passage to support their theology. Theologians such as MacArthur point to Acts 1:1–4 and John 7:14–16, 16:7, arguing that these passages support the conclusion that the disciples did not receive the Holy Spirit till Pentecost.[18]

There might be some merit to the charismatic interpretation if one views this from an exegetical perspective. Jesus did breathe on the disciples, imparting some measure of the Holy Spirit, regardless of whether they used or realized what Jesus had given them. The Holy Spirit was imparted at that time for a purpose. In John 20:22, Jesus speaks to his disciples in the present tense, indicating that it is now and not some later event. Perhaps, the giving of the Spirit here was for life in the Spirit, not empowerment.

Looking at the following verse: John 20:23. Jesus, after saying, "Receive the Holy Spirit" in verse 22, tells his disciples, "If you forgive anyone's sins, their sins are forgiven; if you do not forgive them, they are not forgiven" (John 20:23). Could this be the reason for the giving of the Spirit at this time—for the disciples to be able to forgive those who would persecute them? However, concerning John 20:22, Culpepper asserts, "The disciples receiving the Holy Spirit at this moment experienced new life in the Spirit, but they were still in need of the enduement with power from on high." [19] This would occur on the day of Pentecost, when the outpouring of the Spirit would be given. MacArthur argues, "When the Holy Spirit came at Pentecost, a new order was established. From then on, the Holy Spirit came to every believer at the moment of faith and indwelt the believer in a permanent relationship."[20]

---

18. MacArthur, *Charismatic Chaos*, 176–77.
19. Culpepper, *Charismatic Movement*, 57.
20. MacArthur, *Charismatic Chaos*, 178.

CHAPTER 3: ISSUES THAT DIVIDE

Acts 4:31 seems to provide credence to the charismatic doctrine of the subsequent filling of the Holy Spirit and the baptism of the Holy Spirit. Here in Acts 4:31, Luke conveys that Peter and John were jailed because of their preaching, teaching, and healing of a man (Acts 4:1-22). They spoke with such power, being filled with the Holy Spirit (Acts 4:8). Luke notes that they went back to their people upon their release and told them what had happened (Acts 4:23-30).

Charismatics interpret Acts 4:31 to be a subsequent event, because of what Luke asserts: "After they prayed, the place where they were meeting was shaken. And they were all filled with the Holy Spirit and spoke the word of God boldly." All of this took place after the day of Pentecost, when all the disciples were filled with the Holy Spirit and spoke in tongues.

Derek W. H. Thomas believes that it is part of a sequence of things regarding the Holy Spirit's filling for power to proclaim God's word boldly.[21] However, expository-based preachers would also concur in that this passage refers to an event of the filling of the Holy Spirit, but they would emphasize the power of "prayer." They are asking God for the power of the Holy Spirit for that moment in time to speak his words boldly and to perform miraculous signs and wonders in Jesus' name. Thomas acknowledges, "Luke wants us to see the connection between prayer and the power of the Spirit."[22] However, MacArthur asserts that there is a difference between the Spirit's baptism and the filling of the Spirit. MacArthur's position is that the charismatics' error is in understanding baptism in the Spirit as being filled with the Spirit. He suggests that charismatics are confusing Spirit baptism, which engrafts Christians into the body of Christ, with being filled with the Spirit, which produces active Christian living (see Eph 5:18, 6:11).[23] Understanding these principles concerning the function of the Holy Spirit will only enhance the preaching of both methods.

---

21. Thomas, *Acts*, 105.
22. Thomas, *Acts*, 105.
23. MacArthur, *Charismatic Chaos*, 192.

CHARISMATIC AND EXPOSITORY PREACHING

Charismatics' interpretation of Matt 12:22–31 deals with their understanding of the usage of spiritual gifts, particularly the gift of healing. Charismatics preach that believers possess those gifts that the early church displayed during the time of the apostles. However, expository preachers argue that those gifts ceased with the passing of the apostles. For charismatics, the gifts of the Spirit are still active in this modern age of the church. Many charismatic preachers practice the laying on of hands for healing during their worship service. Margaret Poloma confirms this with her assertion that "the practice of placing hands on the head or shoulder of the person to be healed is a common practice of charismatics when praying for healing."[24] Poloma also acknowledges that the charismatic position on deliverance from evil spirits is a real force in the world but that it is not as strong as the Holy Spirit's positive power in believers' lives.[25]

Mark 16:17–18 is another passage used by charismatics to validate their theology concerning the Holy Spirit and the healing ministry. What charismatics argue is that the church possesses these gifts of the Spirit, which empower the church. Charismatic and expository preachers alike preach with the Holy Spirit's power and acknowledge the work and power of the Spirit in the church. One cannot dismiss the supernatural, because the church moves in the supernatural by the Holy Spirit's power if it is grounded in Christ, the Word of God. MacArthur argues:

> The gift of healing was one of the miraculous sign gifts given to help the apostolic community confirm the authority of the gospel message in the early years of the church. Once the Word of God was complete, the signs ceased. Miraculous signs were no longer needed. The apostles used healing only as a powerful sign to convince people of the validity of the gospel message.[26]

John 16:7–11 is concise in explaining the work and function of the Holy Spirit. Jesus conveys to his disciples that he must go

24. Poloma, *Charismatic Movement*, 93.
25. Poloma, *Charismatic Movement*, 96–97.
26. MacArthur, *Charismatic Chaos*, 215.

CHAPTER 3: ISSUES THAT DIVIDE

back to the Father, who sent him, and if he does not go, the Advocate cannot come. However, he comforts them by letting them know that it is for their benefit that the Advocate will come (the Holy Spirit). Charismatics reference this passage to support their claim that the Holy Spirit is active in believers' lives just as he was in the early church and the apostles. Jesus provides evidence of this claim in John 14:12, where he asserts, "Anyone who has faith in me will do what I have been doing. He will do even greater things than these." The writer of Hebrews assures us that "Jesus Christ is the same yesterday and today and forever" (Heb 13:8).

Paul confirms in 1 Cor 12:27–37 that the body of Christ possesses all the Holy Spirit's spiritual gifts to be used to edify the church, bringing glory to Christ so that the world may believe. Nowhere in the New Testament does it confirm that the spiritual gifts ceased.[27] Therefore, what is the main point John is conveying in John 16:7–11? In his interpretation, renowned scholar Elmer Towns asserts:

> Jesus finishes the Upper Room Discourse by pointing His disciples to the work of the Holy Spirit. Since the Holy Spirit is sent to meet a need, Jesus reminds them that they will be sustained by the Holy Spirit's presence. The disciples had difficulty conceiving of life without Jesus, but as He explained, His departure was to their advantage.[28]

Because of Jesus' departure, the disciples gain the Helper (the Holy Spirit).[29] Charismatics argue that this solidifies their theological position on the work and actions of the Holy Spirit. Especially coming from Jesus, this confirms the Holy Spirit's importance and continuation in believers and in the church's mission. Not only do charismatics insist that in every aspect of ministry in the church, the Holy Spirit is active, but those who are firm in expository preaching also concur in that the Holy Spirit must lead and guide

---

27. Culpepper, *Charismatic Movement*, 85.
28. Towns, *Gospel of John*, 159–60.
29. Towns, *Gospel of John*, 159–60.

one's ministry when it comes to preaching. Bill Bennett quotes Vines, who concurs with this argument:

> We must seek the Spirit's anointing. Ask Him to come on you and your message. Allow Him to manifest His power in and through you. Never be satisfied with anything less in your sermon delivery. You may not always experience the power of the Holy Spirit upon your preaching in equal measure. For reasons in the realm of the mysterious, there are times when the anointing comes upon us in larger measure than at other times... But there should be such a surrender of life to the Spirit that every time we preach, there is evidence of God's blessings upon us.[30]

Therefore, there is an agreement between the two preaching methods regarding the Holy Spirit's work in preaching, in the church, and in the believer's life. The Holy Spirit must be active, because it brings validation to one's preaching, ministry, and the gospel. Only the Holy Spirit will illuminate the Father and the Son to believers and the world.

The charismatic theological approach to preaching becomes more profound when viewed from Paul's theological perspective in Rom 15:19 and 1 Cor 2:4. Paul conveys that his entire ministry, through his preaching, signs, and wonders, was accomplished by the power of the Holy Spirit for the sole purpose of making Christ known to the Jews and especially to the gentiles. Paul acknowledges that his message and preaching were not with wise and persuasive words but with a demonstration of the Spirit's power (1 Cor 2:4). Mark Taylor asserts in his commentary on 1 Corinthians that "Paul's preaching was effective for God's purposes because of the empowerment of the Spirit. The Spirit bore witness to the truth of the message."[31]

Paul's theological position regarding the Holy Spirit's work is based on the argument that what they are preaching and doing is by the Holy Spirit's power. Paul confirms throughout his Pauline

---

30. Jerry Vines, qtd. in Bill Bennett, "The Secret of Preaching with Power," in Akin et al., *Text-Driven Preaching*, 57.

31. Taylor, *New American Commentary*, 81.

CHAPTER 3: ISSUES THAT DIVIDE

discourse that it is by the Holy Spirit's power that signs and wonders are being done through him so that unbelievers should believe in Christ. Charismatics, without a doubt, display charisma in their delivery of the gospel message, so many gravitate to them. However, expository preachers possess this same kind of charisma and experience tremendous growth in their churches.

As Kilian McDonnell notes, "In the New Testament, charisms are operations or manifestations of the Holy Spirit in and for the Christian community."[32] Thus, charismatics and expository preachers can agree "that to each is given the manifestation of the Spirit for the common good" (1 Cor 12:7). Charismatic and expository preachers must possess the Holy Spirit to validate their preaching. McDonnell acknowledges, "Like the Holy Spirit itself, the charisms are gifts; they are given by God and are not something a person merits."[33] Therefore, charismatics and expository preachers have a great deal in common regarding the Holy Spirit's work and function in their preaching ministry and other ministries in the local church.

First Corinthians 12–14 is at the core of charismatic theology, its preaching approach, and its doctrinal teaching. Paul's focus is on the spiritual gifts imparted by the Holy Spirit to the body of believers. Paul wanted to correct them on their understanding of spiritual gifts. Paul wanted them to understand the usage of spiritual gifts and come together in unity, caring for the Christian community through the love of Christ.

In 1 Cor 12, Paul emphasizes unity, community, many parts of the body, and the priority of love within the church. As Preben Vang points out, "God empowers his people by his Spirit for the common good of his community, not as a personal favor to the individual. When individuals use their God-granted power for personal gain, they act like pagans attempting to manipulate their idol, God."[34] Charismatic preaching must stand on the solid principles of biblical teachings about Christ and the salvation of humanity.

---

32. McDonnell, *Charismatics Renewal*, 6.
33. McDonnell, *Charismatics Renewal*, 6.
34. Vang, *1 Corinthians*, 160.

CHARISMATIC AND EXPOSITORY PREACHING

Many charismatic preachers have lost their way by preaching more on spiritual experiences and the material things many seek than preaching to live by God's word. God's word says his desire is for us to prosper (see Prov 13:21). Our Christian experience is not based on material things: "But seek first his kingdom and his righteousness, and all these things will be given to you as well" (Matt 6:33). In 1 Cor 13, Paul explains the importance of love that supersedes any spiritual gift. Paul viewed love as the ultimate force in the church; without it, all spiritual gifts are useless.

From Paul's theological perspective, love unifies the church and controls the gifts' usage. With love, the gifts are of excellent service to the church, and without it, the gifts are in vain (see 1 Cor 13:1–13), because first and foremost, God is love. As Gordon D. Fee notes, "Paul sets out to put their zeal for tongues within a broader ethical context that will ultimately disallow uninterpreted tongues in the assembly. That context is love for others over against self-interest, which in chapter 14 will be specified in terms of building up the church."[35] By love, the Spirit's gifts will be effective in the church, especially in preaching. In 1 Cor 14, Paul confirms the importance of love and true Christian worship being done decently and in order among believers in the church, not denying the spiritual gifts but instructing believers in how to use the gifts properly in worship with love. Vang notes:

> Unless Christ's loving character becomes evident in the use and application of any and all of the Spirit's gifts, their practice becomes worthless for God's kingdom and mere demonstration of Christian immaturity . . . Although the Spirit's gifts do not grant status to their recipients, the gifts that benefit and build up Christ's community are of greater significance and value than those used only for the personal benefit of the individual . . . Christian worship gatherings must be conducted in an orderly fashion to avoid confusion and ensure that the character of Christ is clearly portrayed throughout the service.[36]

---

35. Fee, *God's Empowering Presence*, 198.
36. Vang, *1 Corinthians*, 180–92.

CHAPTER 3: ISSUES THAT DIVIDE

Although there are disagreements between these two preaching methods, if these issues are debated in love, letting the Holy Spirit intercede, the outcome would be unification, because the same Spirit dwells in both charismatic and expository preaching. Therefore, charismatic and expository preachers find commonality in love through the Holy Spirit's precious guidance. As Wayne A. Grudem explains, "At Pentecost, with the beginning of the new creation in Christ, it is the Holy Spirit who comes to grant power to the church (Acts 1:8; 2:4, 17–18 NIV) . . . the Holy Spirit empowers, he purifies, he reveals, and he unifies."[37]

If the Holy Spirit empowers both preaching methods, then there is no doubt that the two can be solidified. The future of preaching would transcend the way the word of God is delivered in contemporary worship services because of the Holy Spirit's involvement; the Spirit of God will only unify, because God is not divided. The God we serve is a God of order and not division. I concur with Geoffrey Stevenson: "[In] the preaching of the future, the Bible will surely continue to occupy a crucial place. As witness to the unique revelatory and redemptive acts of God, it is irreplaceable, and will continue to be so throughout this present age of gospel proclamation, until God's kingdom is consummated."[38] Regardless of the preaching methods that charismatic and expository preachers use, God's word and Spirit will always be the door through which preachers of the gospel must enter.

In Gal 3:5, Paul rebukes the Galatians for yielding to false doctrines and turning from the true gospel they had heard and converted to when they chose to follow Christ. Many biblical scholars perceive the charismatic movement as a situation similar to that of the Galatians. Paul's question to the Galatians is the following: "After beginning with the Spirit, are you now trying to attain your goal by human effort?" (Gal 3:3). However, in Gal 3:5, Paul asks the question, "Does God give you his Spirit and work miracles among you because you observed the law, or because you believe what you heard?" (Gal 3:5).

37. Grudem, *Systematic Theology*, 635.
38. Stevenson, *Future of Preaching*, 84.

This same question must be asked of the charismatic movement because of the tremendous criticism it receives from advocates against their interpretation of the scriptures concerning receiving the Holy Spirit. MacArthur criticizes the charismatic movement, because "it is scriptural to be concerned about whether our brothers and sisters are walking in the truth. Although it may not seem very loving to some, the Bible is clear that we are to speak the truth in love (Eph 4:15)."[39] The Holy Spirit guides all preaching, because it identifies the truth of God's word. It is incumbent on practitioners of both preaching methods to succumb to the Holy Spirit's power to be valuable models for advancing the gospel and the growth of the church. Charismatics and expository preachers must speak God's truth, not what people want to hear but what people need to hear. Truth is another element that connects both preaching methods—that is, preaching the truth.

Combining Both Preaching Methods

From an exegetical viewpoint, expository scholars view the charismatic interpretation of the scriptures concerning speaking in tongues—that they are evidence of being filled with the Holy Spirit—to be in error. However, combining expository and charismatic preaching is theologically sound. However, the approach must use exegesis and hermeneutical skills vigorously. Peter Adam asserts, "Preaching is best understood as one part of the ministry of the Word, and it derives its theological character from the biblical basis for all aspects of the ministry of the Word."[40] Therefore, every word that comes from the preacher's mouth must be the unadulterated word of God. To combine the two preaching methods, one first looks at the three great theological foundations of preaching.[41] First, the preacher must believe that God has spoken; second, that his words remain powerful and life changing; and

---

39. MacArthur, *Charismatic Chaos*, 245.
40. Adam, *Speaking God's Words*, 15.
41. Adam, *Speaking God's Words*, 15.

CHAPTER 3: ISSUES THAT DIVIDE

third, there can be no ministry of the word without the historical revelation of God's word.[42]

Charismatic preachers project a particular image or charisma to their audience or congregation when conveying God's word. Also, expository preachers are charismatic as well when empowered by the Holy Spirit. Thus, both preaching methods are empowered by the Holy Spirit to convey the word of God with power that convicts the souls of unbelievers and believers alike. Jerry Vines and Jim Shaddix, concerning the Holy Spirit's influence in the pulpit, suggest:

> The message of the Bible is communicated through a twofold medium: the Holy Spirit and a human personality. From outset to conclusion, preaching is the communication of the Holy Spirit. John Knox said, "true preaching from start to finish is the work of the Holy Spirit." He inspired the Word we preach. He illuminates our understanding as to its meaning. He anoints our communication of it. He enlightens the minds of listeners. He convicts their hearts and prompts them to respond. Preaching is the Holy Spirit event. If He is left out, preaching does not happen.[43]

The charismatic position has always been to focus on the Holy Spirit and the gifts with which he empowers believers within the church to enhance the gospel message. One can also assert that fundamentally, expository preachers' focus is on the Holy Spirit, so both preaching methods have this commonality. The Holy Spirit connects both preaching methods and illuminates such a charisma that the word of God comes forth with power that touches the congregation's hearts and souls, bringing forth acceptance of Christ as their Savior.

Therefore, observing these preaching methods for research has revealed that charismatic preachers' ministries surpass those of expository preachers. What has been observed is not so much the context of the message but its delivery. Charismatic preachers

---

42. Adam, *Speaking God's Words*, 15.
43. Vines and Shaddix, *Power in the Pulpit*, 25.

come forth with such flair that they capture the audience from the very beginning with their gifts, be it singing or that charisma of speech to interact with the congregation, at the same time invoking the power of the Holy Spirit to lead and guide them as they convey the word of God. Even when the charismatic preacher proceeds to bring God's word, the atmosphere is so energized that he or she need not say anything else because of the experience that is taking place.

However, expository preachers that possess the same talents or gifts as charismatic preachers exhibit that same type of flair, allowing the Holy Spirit to use them in a compelling way to experience the same kind of response. From R. Scott Pace's perspective: "We all have favorite preachers whom we admire. Whether because of their dynamic delivery, spiritual passion, or a clear explanation of the biblical text, certain preachers inspire us."[44] He goes on to explain, "We may not be able to pinpoint a specific attribute that resonates most with us because good preaching involves a combination of essential factors, both human and divine."[45] These are the two factors that combine both charismatic and expository preaching. Both are human and divine; however, they must preach the unadulterated word of God.

Integrating both preaching methods requires understanding that one's theology of preaching and convictions regarding Scripture compels one to kneel humbly before God with boldness and stand with confidence by his Spirit and proclaim the word of the Lord.[46] Whether charismatic or expository, preachers must keep the primary goal in mind: to clarify or apply a textual truth.[47] Preachers must stand on the fact that scriptural truth is spiritual truth, regardless of the method.[48] The preacher's role is to communicate

---

44. Pace, *Preaching by the Book*, 3.
45. Pace, *Preaching by the Book*, 3.
46. Pace, *Preaching by the Book*, 12.
47. Pace, *Preaching by the Book*, 80.
48. Pace, *Preaching by the Book*, 81.

CHAPTER 3: ISSUES THAT DIVIDE

God's truth clearly and forcefully so that no one is confused but understands what God is saying to them.[49]

Charismatic and expository preaching methods are subject to the rigorous process of exegesis, hermeneutics, and homiletics. Although charismatics may be considered in error on specific passages in the Scriptures, this can be mitigated with a sound interpretation of the word of God. As Jerry Vines and Jim Shaddix assert, "The very nature of preaching demands that the preacher applies the process of exposition."[50]

However, what is lacking with some expository preachers is the Holy Spirit's fire, which gives divine power to the oracle, bringing forth God's message. It is the Holy Spirit that moves and empowers the church. The Holy Spirit only will reveal Christ and God's will for humanity and his church. Therefore, as David L. Allen asserts concerning text-driven preaching regardless of preaching styles:

> The method of preparing text-driven sermons is ungirded by certain biblical and theological convictions... the biblical and theological foundation for all preaching is the fact that God has revealed Himself. God is a God who speaks. Hebrews 1:1 states it clearly, "God, having spoken in times past to the fathers by the prophets in many portions and in many ways, has in these last day spoken to us by his Son."[51]

Conclusion

The sole purpose of this research is to determine if charismatic and expository preaching methods can be integrated as a sound preaching method. The theological foundation of preaching derives from the preacher's convictions about God and his divine self-disclosure

49. Pace, *Preaching by the Book*, 94.
50. Vines and Shaddix, *Power in the Pulpit*, 27.
51. David L. Allen, "Preparing a Text-Driven Sermon," in Akin et al., *Text-Driven Preaching*, 101.

CHARISMATIC AND EXPOSITORY PREACHING

of himself in Scripture.[52] Both charismatics and expository preachers share this same conviction in their approach to preaching God's word. That is, as declared by the Scriptures: "That there is only one true God who exists in three persons, the Father, the Son, and the Holy Spirit (Deut 6:4; Isa 46:9; Matt 28:19; 2 Cor 13:14)."[53] Every preacher must hold to this truth in proclaiming God's word to the world. Although the charismatic preacher's approach may differ from that of expository preachers, the end is the same, which is that Christ died, was buried, and rose on the third day, and he and the Father are one with the Holy Spirit, empowering the church and helping people recognize the divine Godhead.

Therefore, charismatic and expository preaching combined are even more effective in conveying the word of God, because the manifestation of the gifts of the Holy Spirit and sound biblical teaching will draw people to Christ. Although many biblical scholars point to errors in the charismatic interpretation of Scripture concerning the Holy Spirit and the gifts the Spirit provides for the church, they cannot deny that the Holy Spirit empowers charismatics and expository preachers. Therefore, commonality cannot be argued concerning these two preaching methods; they both depend on the Holy Spirit's help and both preach Christ being crucified, being buried, and rising from the dead on the third day. Upon this confession is based the gospel that all preachers preach to the world and to their congregations.

This research reveals that charismatic and expository preaching are intertwined, bound by the same fundamental principles of preaching: "Preaching is textual," "preaching is contextual," "preaching is theological," "preaching speaks to the mind of the listener," and "preaching speaks to the heart of the listener."[54] Charismatic and expository preaching methods hinge upon these principles. Recognizing the Holy Spirit's work—from which both charismatic and expository preachers receive their divine power—is standard, because it is God's Spirit that speaks through them. The

---

52. Pace, *Preaching by the Book*, 5.
53. Pace, *Preaching by the Book*, 5.
54. Schmit, "Key Principles of Preaching," paras. 1, 4, 6, 7, 8.

CHAPTER 3: ISSUES THAT DIVIDE

gifts of the Holy Spirit are crucial in the life of the church. The Holy Spirit's power that manifested itself on the day of Pentecost (Acts 2) is still empowering the church today. When the power of the Holy Spirit comes upon them, all Christians are charismatic, because it is the power of God that is at work proclaiming the supremacy of his Son, Jesus Christ. To quote R. Scott Pace:

> We must first recognize that the Spirit is the divine agent of inspiration. Scripture was conceived by the work of the Spirit through the biblical writers. By the Holy Spirit, human authors recorded God's message in a supernatural way that incorporated their knowledge, skills, personality, and experience while preserving the divine nature of His written Word (2 Peter 1:19–21). Through His work of inspiration, the Scriptures reveal God (2 Tim 3:16) and are a living and powerful, two-edged sword that cuts with the precision of a surgical scalpel (Heb 4:12). The same Holy Spirit who inspired Scripture also works in us as the divine agent of interpretation . . . the Spirit is able to help us interpret them faithfully and accurately.[55]

There is still tremendous work and research to be done regarding charismatic and expository preaching methods, particularly around the doctrine of the Holy Spirit. These two preaching methods are formally intertwined and can effectively advance the gospel and the church's growth. For instance, understanding the role of the Holy Spirit in preaching and in the church is necessary for all ministers of the gospel to be effective in their ministries. Preachers that are charismatic or expository should possess vast knowledge of pneumatology (doctrine of the Holy Spirit), since the Holy Spirit is at work in the preaching process. In every avenue of ministry in the church, the Holy Spirit is active, providing the necessary power for those whom God has called to particular ministries to carry out his divine will and purpose successfully. There is a more in-depth conversation about and study in pneumatology within the ecclesia today because of the charismatic movement. Elmer Towns provides clarity; he asserts that "the primary reason

---

55. Pace, *Preaching by the Book*, 7.

CHARISMATIC AND EXPOSITORY PREACHING

for the renewal of interest in the Holy Spirit is the contemporary charismatic movement and the emphasis of that movement on the miraculous sign gifts of the New Testament."[56]

From Towns's viewpoint, opposition against the charismatic movement chooses to disregard the movement as a faddish enthusiasm and a satanic attempt to duplicate the temporary phenomena of the first century.[57] In fact, the charismatic movement should be complemented, and praise should be given to God because of this new recognition of his Spirit, which, in this contemporary church, has been less talked about in worship services—even, some would argue, neglected. The opinion of others in the field of biblical study concerning the charismatic movement has led others into immense research on the doctrine of the Holy Spirit.

For both charismatic and expository preachers, when the Holy Spirit comes upon the orator, there is such power given to the preacher, enabling them to speak with clarity and boldness, illuminating unique charisma that captivates the audience or congregation. The Spirit of God provides the preacher with confidence in conveying God's word, emboldening them in the act of preaching. Therefore, whether with charismatic or expository preachers, the Spirit performs a distinct role of illumination in the lives of all preachers of the gospel and the lives of all believers.[58] It is terrific to know that these two preaching methods are connected by the Holy Spirit, regardless of the difference in interpretation of specific Scripture passages.

When the Holy Spirit impregnates the oracle of God, there is an anointing projecting from the pulpit that fills the sanctuary of God with his presence. Forbes asserts, "If we preach out of the experience of the anointing such as is described in Jesus the Christ, and if we appreciate the nurturing that shapes our lives, and if we experience the Spirit as a collaborator in the process of

---

56. Towns, *Theology for Today*, 262.
57. Towns, *Theology for Today*, 262.
58. Towns, *Theology for Today*, 98.

CHAPTER 3: ISSUES THAT DIVIDE

normal preparation, we can expect to receive the text message that is sent by God."[59]

Regardless of the method, preachers must be filled with the Spirit of God, because the Lord has called them to preach the word to his people and the lost. Charismatics and expository preachers both drink from the same Spirit. Thus, being connected as one is what combines the two methods of preaching the Holy Spirit; without the Spirit, they are distant strangers.

59. Forbes, *Holy Spirit & Preaching*, 83.

Chapter 4: Research Data Analysis

Purpose of This Study

The purpose of this research is to conduct a case study on charismatic and expository preaching to determine if these two preaching methods can be integrated to formulate a sound biblical preaching method that will be effective in spreading the gospel to the world, in its effect on the worship service, and in producing growth in the local church.

This case study's implementation revealed that charismatic and expository preaching are intertwined in their approach to delivering God's word to his people and the world. From the data obtained, both preaching methods are guided by the Holy Spirit's divine power, as conveyed by the pastors and deacon chairpersons interviewed.

However, there are theological issues concerning the charismatic interpretation of Scripture regarding the Holy Spirit's work in the believer's life at the point of conversion. Their stance is that of a second filling of the Holy Spirit in the believer's life after conversion, which—from a charismatic interpretation—is a "baptism of the Holy Spirit." According to charismatics, this event happens after the believer's conversion, empowering them for service in the body of Christ.

Another theological issue that this case study revealed was the charismatic position on speaking in tongues (glossolalia) and the Spirit's other gifts. Many charismatics believe that when a believer speaks in tongues, this is the ultimate evidence of being filled with

CHAPTER 4: RESEARCH DATA ANALYSIS

the Holy Spirit. Nonetheless, the interviews and questionnaires conducted for this case study involved pastors, deacon chairpersons, and three members from each church. Unfortunately, because of this historic, deadly pandemic of COVID-19, which has devastated this great nation, much of this research was hindered by the virus; only three churches could participate. Nonetheless, some significant research conducted within these churches provided tremendous input on this case study's issues. These three churches offered valuable information for comparing the two preaching methods and the highly debated topics in the theological sphere of biblical research that separate the two preaching styles.

Through vigorous hermeneutical and exegetical research, there can be a clarification of the theological and biblical issues dividing charismatic and expository preachers. This study's results with the pastors, deacon chairpersons, and three church members from each church confirmed this theory. The case study can provide a path for the unification of these two preaching methods.

The pastors and deacon chairpersons interviewed were asked five questions concerning their thoughts on the Holy Spirit's work and the gifts and empowerment the Holy Spirit bestows on believers. For instance, the gift of speaking in tongues (glossolalia), laying on of hands, and the Holy Spirit's work during the worship service. The participants were asked to give their perspectives from a charismatic and expository viewpoint. The three church members from each church were also asked to answer ten questions in a questionnaire on their views on the Holy Spirit's work in the church and their lives.

The participants' responses were invigorating, because they supported this case study's hypothesis that charismatic and expository preaching can be integrated as a sound preaching method. These results will be conveyed later in this chapter. However, not surprisingly, many of the participants expressed the desire to experience the manifestation of the Holy Spirit during the worship service. Christians hunger for that Pentecostal experience that soothes the soul and touches the heart; they long to feel the awesomeness of God's power. We need that experience in the church today.

Review of Case-Study Research by Chapter

Chapter 1 consists of the introduction, ministry context, statement of the problem, statement of delimitations, statement of limitations, theoretical basis, and statement of methodology, as well as a review of books, journals, and Scripture references to help support this case study's thesis.

Chapter 2 explored the question of what precisely charismatic and expository preaching is. Chapter 2 sought to define the two preaching methods and reveal the theological issues that divide the two by analyzing the scriptures used by charismatics to justify their theological understanding of the Bible's messages and formulate their doctrine. It also explored expository preachers' perspectives on those same theological issues and their analysis of charismatic interpretations, which were scripturally incorrect from their view.

Chapter 3 involved the research methods that were taken to address this research's issues, providing details of the approach that would be used in arriving at some understanding of the problems outlined regarding charismatic and expository preaching. At the center of the debate is the Holy Spirit's work and the spiritual gifts bestowed upon believers in their spiritual walk, which biblical scholars and theologians alike view as a "pneumatology" issue (doctrine of the Holy Spirit). Chapter 3 acknowledges that advocates against charismatic doctrine and preaching reveal that charismatics are in error in their interpretation of the scriptures concerning the Holy Spirit's divine function at the believer's conversion and in their interpretation that the distribution of the spiritual gifts is evidence of a "subsequential event" of the "baptism of the Holy Spirit."

Chapter 4 reveals the results of the research done. In this chapter, the interviews and questionnaires will be analyzed and reviewed to draw conclusions from the data obtained and make recommendations to add to this subject's study. The goal is also to implement a strategy that may consolidate both preaching methods.

CHAPTER 4: RESEARCH DATA ANALYSIS

Chapter 5 is the conclusion of the research project. Within this chapter's context, I will make recommendations to this field of study, because a tremendous amount of work can be added.

Review of the Results from Interviews and Questionnaires

Interviewing these pastors, deacon chairpersons, and church members from each church on charismatic and expository preaching was very informative for all who participated. Some of the church members were not knowledgeable of the terms "charismatic" and "expository preaching." However, each pastor educated their members on the terminology and doctrine of the charismatic and expository preaching approaches. The pastors helping their congregants understand these preaching methods enabled them to understand what their pastors and deacon chairpersons were doing in their preaching and devotional services. Now, they could categorize these methods as expository or charismatic.

Approximately fifteen people participated in this case study on charismatic and expository preaching. As stated earlier in this chapter, because of the COVID-19 pandemic, the research had to be scaled back to only three participating churches. Therefore, from each church, the pastor and deacon chairperson were interviewed and three members from each church completed a questionnaire. The interviews with the pastors and deacon chairpersons took around thirty minutes to conduct with each interviewee; they were pretty insightful about charismatic and expository preaching. They were asked five questions, and these are the responses from the pastor and deacon chairperson of each church. The results of these interviews show that each pastor and deacon chairperson were knowledgeable of both preaching methods and aware of the Holy Spirit's role from both perspectives.

CHARISMATIC AND EXPOSITORY PREACHING

Analysis of Interview Responses

Interviews with Pastor Spencer and Deacon Sherman (New Hope Missionary Church)

Pastor W. Spencer and Deacon G. Sherman of New Hope Missionary Church were the first to be interviewed.

Pastor W. Spencer was asked first to give his overall thoughts on the subject of charismatic and expository preaching. His response was as follows:

> The only thing in our preaching is sound doctrine, and this is how it should be. However, from a charismatic perspective, it is all for show. If we look closely at Peter's first sermon (Acts 2:14–36), it was [centered] strictly on the fact that Jesus died and was buried and on the third day rose. When one becomes a believer, it is the word of God that pierces the heart. Therefore, Peter's preaching in Acts 2 was to bring nonbelievers to Christ. That is why Paul had to admonish the believers in the church of Corinth (1 Cor 1–12), because what they were doing was incorrect. Therefore, the main goal, regardless of spiritual gifts, is to preach God's word.

Pastor Spencer is, by all definitions, an expository preacher. His position is that God's word has sole authority. Pastor Spencer's thoughts on charismatic preaching concur with other pastors' views, such as Jerry Vines and John MacArthur. For instance, Jerry Vines argues that charismatics put more emphasis on feelings and experience, which, from his perspective, is "the Achilles heel of the Charismatic approach to doctrine and discipleship."[1] Vines's view is that Christians must "approach the Bible as the final source of authority."[2]

Pastor Spencer's theological position is the same as that of Vines—that it is God's word that Christians must adhere to and follow. However, Pastor Spencer accepts charismatic preaching in its totality but states that it is all for show for some preachers, from

---

1. Mohler, "Charismatic Movement," para. 8. These are Mohler's words.
2. Jerry Vines, qtd. in Mohler, "Charismatic Movement," para. 8.

CHAPTER 4: RESEARCH DATA ANALYSIS

what he has seen. Pastor Spencer noted that the same Spirit that empowers him also empowers a charismatic preacher. His skepticism is due to his observation that some charismatic preachers are only showboating with the gospel message. Sadly, many believers are captivated by this approach and miss the big picture—that it is about leading the lost to Christ, regardless of spiritual gifts.

The complete list of questions is available in Appendix A: Research Interview Questions. The following are the responses from the interviewees.

Interview with Pastor Spencer

Pastor Spencer's answer to these questions was expository based. However, because this is the pastor of my home church, I decided only to summarize his response to the research questions:

Pastor Spencer's answer to these questions was straightforward. He strictly and unapologetically stands on the authority of God's word. He believes that when anyone enters the sanctuary on Sunday mornings for worship service, there should be an expectation of hearing God's word for empowerment and spiritual change. They should leave the service changed and empowered by the Holy Spirit. He acknowledges that God's word and the help of the Holy Spirit enable the church to carry out its primary duty of being a witness to the word of God and spreading the gospel message.

Pastor Spencer asserted that although the Spirit's gifts are present in the church, one should not put them before God's word. "We do not need to speak in tongues or lay hands on the believers to show that we are filled with the Spirit. If we live according to God's Word, it will show that His Spirit is dwelling in you, and if you have any of the gifts, then that is a blessing as well for God's glory." Pastor Spencer does not dismiss the charismatic movement but feels that it has its place if used correctly, not emphasizing the Spirit's gifts and experiences but focusing more on God's word; this is where spiritual growth occurs.

CHARISMATIC AND EXPOSITORY PREACHING

Interview with Deacon Sherman

The second interview was with Deacon G. Sherman of New Hope Missionary Baptist Church, where he has been a deacon for twenty years. The same approach was taken in interviewing him. He was asked to give his thoughts on the case-study topic, and he answered the following:

> Both charismatic and expository preachers are in line with God. Both methods can coexist. Although preachers must be straight with God—if not, they get into trouble. The preacher must be real with God's word and live it as well. You can preach the word and be straightforward with God by living out what you preach. Preachers [have] got to do what the Lord commands and do it decently and in order. If you are doing what the Lord commands, he will provide the tools you need to complete the task he has called you to do. The gifts of the Spirit will be there for the usage of that task. Both charismatics and expository preachers possess the gifts of the Spirit, and believers as well.

Deacon Sherman's position is that all ministers are charismatic and possess spiritual gifts if they are humble and obedient to God's word. Deacon Sherman sees no difference in charismatic and expository preaching. For him, the minister must be faithful to God and his word. As he said, "It does not matter if you have spiritual gifts, but if you are devoted to Christ, these blessings will come to empower you for what God has called you to do."

Deacon Sherman's answers to the interview questions were along the same lines as those of his pastor, Walter Spencer.

Summary of interview questions: Deacon Sherman's responses to the interview questions centered on the love of God's word. Every Sunday morning, he expects to hear a word from the Lord; the pastor must present God's word truthfully and not with charismatic antics, because if one is faithful to God's word, the Holy Spirit will reveal it. If the preacher is right with God and in tune with God, the Holy Spirit will move. The Holy Spirit is not the problem; the Holy Spirit is within us. When we are faithful to God, the Holy Spirit will lead and guide us. Nonetheless, one must believe in God's word. Sherman's total theology is based on God's word as authoritative. From his perspective, no one needs to speak in tongues or show any spiritual gifts; if God's word is put first and we live by it, the Spirit of God will shine through believers. In conclusion, Deacon Sherman accepts charismatic preaching. He believes that if a preacher is faithful to God and his walk is in submission to Christ, both preaching methods can coexist.

Interviews with Pastor Watson and Deacon Ford (Mount Olive Baptist Church)

Interview with Pastor Watson

Pastor L. Watson of Mount Olive Baptist Church is a man after God's own heart. He has pastored at Mount Olive Baptist Church for over twenty years. He is one pastor that balances the preaching method of both. Although he is an expository preacher in method, he can be very charismatic when the Spirit engulfs him in his presentation. He was asked to elaborate on his thoughts on charismatic and expository preaching as they pertained to the case-study thesis to find out if these two preaching methods can become a solidified method for preaching. His response was as follows:

> I do not think that charismatic and expository preaching can coexist as a combined preaching method. The reason why is that charismatic and expository preaching, from my perspective, are different for two reasons. First, expository preaching lets the word speak for itself; and second, charismatic preaching is based on one's understanding of what the Scriptures may be saying. When it comes to God's word, my opinion is not what I think the Bible conveys to its readers.[3] Charismatics read into

---

3. What Pastor Watson is trying to say is that he can't claim his opinion as the authoritative interpretation of what the Bible is saying. We must stay within the boundaries of the original intent of the author.

the Bible their understanding of what the Scriptures are saying on a particular subject. Their faith and belief are rooted in their experience and spiritual gifts, be it genuine or not. However, the same Spirit flows through both charismatics and expository preachers, empowering the preacher to proclaim the gospel message.

Pastor Watson's theological position is like Pastor Spencer's. Both pastors hold to a foundationally expository preaching method. They take time to approach their sermons by preparing hermeneutically, exegetically, and homiletically in dealing with God's word. Pastor Watson's answers to the interview questions reflect his theological position on the research subjects. Below are Pastor Watson's responses to the interview questions.

Q 1. What are your expectations on Sunday mornings when entering the sanctuary for worship?

Pastor Watson: "On Sunday mornings, I expect a real understanding of the gospel that will come alive in the flock that I lead."

Q 2. What are your thoughts on the Holy Spirit? Do you look more to the movement of the Holy Spirit to validate your spirituality in living out God's word as conveyed in Scripture?

Pastor Watson: "For me, it is to live out God's word as conveyed in Scripture to validate my spirituality.[4] To look at the Holy Spirit to validate my spirituality means I would have to rely on the Spirit's gifts, which means I would have to display that speaking in tongues is some manifestation of the spiritual gifts. Whereas, with God's word, all that is required is to be obedient and live as his word indicates. Therefore, I must do what God's word conveys. See, the Holy Spirit reveals those signs at that moment for God's purpose, but living out God's word is an ever-going process."

---

4. In other words, it is the word of God that validates our spirituality as we live according to the word, which is a everyday process for the believer. The Holy Spirit leads and guides believers in living out God's word.

CHAPTER 4: RESEARCH DATA ANALYSIS

Q 3. Do you think that the gifts of the Spirit, such as speaking in tongues and signs and wonders such as the laying on of hands for healing, must be manifested in the church during worship services to give credence that God is still actively empowering the church other than by the power of his word?

Pastor Watson: "No, I think that God's word is manifested in our lives as evidence. That is why I do not feel that charismatic and expository preaching can coexist as a sound preaching method."

Q 4. Do you feel that a believer must speak in tongues as evidence of being filled with the Spirit?

Pastor Watson: "No, because that is another wall that divides; this subject keeps charismatic and expository preachers apart. However, I am not suggesting that the spiritual gifts are not significant, because they are when it comes to the church; it is the Holy Spirit that empowers. Nonetheless, I do not think speaking in tongues is the central evidence of being filled with the Spirit. Not all Christians speak in tongues. The undisputed evidence is love, that gift of love that Christ spoke of, and Paul also (see Luke 6:27–36, John 13:34–35, 1 Cor 13–14). All Christians must possess the gift of love."

Q 5. Do you, as a believer, feel that God's word is sufficient, or is there a need for the miraculous manifestation of the supernatural in the life of the believer to prove being filled with the Spirit?

Pastor Watson: "God's word is enough. God's word does it all; the word manifests itself in believers' lives, and it achieves God's purpose."

Interview with Deacon Ford

The interview with Deacon W. Ford of Mount Olive Baptist Church was informative regarding his theological views of charismatic and expository preaching. Deacon Ford gravitates more toward seeing the Holy Spirit move in his life and in the lives of others in his church. He is more in line with charismatic doctrine and preaching and experiencing the Holy Spirit's gifts in the believer. Below are Deacon Ford's responses to the interview questions.

> Q 1. What are your expectations on Sunday mornings when entering the sanctuary for worship?

> Deacon Ford: "On Sunday mornings when entering the sanctuary for worship, it is a time to be still for me. I expect the Holy Spirit to show up and fill the sanctuary with God's glory. On that morning, I look forward to hearing a Spirit-filled word conveyed by the pastor, bringing God's word with power from the Holy Spirit. With this power-filled word, we all can be filled and replenished for another week's journey."

> Q 2. What are your thoughts on the Holy Spirit? Do you look more to the movement of the Holy Spirit to validate your spirituality in living out God's word as conveyed in Scripture?

> Deacon Ford: "First and foremost, the Holy Spirit is what Jesus left us as he went back to the Father (John 16:5–16). It is hard to call yourself a Christian if you are not filled with the Holy Spirit. When the Holy Spirit is upon you, you cannot be still; you've got to move, even shouting out amen, clapping your hands or something, all because it is the Holy Spirit at work in you. God's word is authoritative, but I need to feel the presence of the Holy Spirit."

> Q 3. Do you think that the gifts of the Spirit, such as speaking in tongues and signs and wonders such as the laying on of hands for healing, must be manifested in the church during worship services to give credence that God is still actively empowering the church other than by the power of his word?

> Deacon Ford: "We know what the Bible says about speaking in tongues. We must have faith in Christ to have any of these spiritual gifts. First and foremost, you must believe. If you do not believe and have no faith, it is all in vain. You are like a ship without a sail."

CHAPTER 4: RESEARCH DATA ANALYSIS

Q 4. Do you feel that a believer must speak in tongues as evidence of being filled with the Spirit?

Deacon Ford: "No, you do not have to speak in tongues. Paul said it is better not to speak in tongues if it is not going to edify the church (see 1 Cor 14). Besides, no one knows what you are saying when speaking in tongues. Only God knows."

Q 5. Do you, as a believer, feel that God's word is sufficient, or is there a need for the miraculous manifestation of the supernatural in the life of the believer to prove being filled with the Spirit?

Deacon Ford: "I am seventy-four years old. God and his Spirit have blessed me, because the Holy Spirit has guided me through life, especially the difficult times. The Spirit of God has changed me; it turned my life around. Therefore, for me, it takes both God's word and the manifestation of the supernatural at certain times in your life on this Christian journey. Sometimes, believers need to see and even experience the supernatural move of God in our lives and the church. However, his word kept me grounded and in comfort. If we allow God's word and his Spirit to guide us, the evidence of being filled with his Spirit is transparent."

Interview Summary for Pastor Watson and Deacon Ford

Pastor L. Watson and Deacon W. Ford of Mount Olive Baptist Church presented different theological responses to the interview questions on charismatic and expository preaching. The interview questions formulated were to obtain their understanding of the Holy Spirit's work and God's word in the preaching process and worship in the church. The purpose of the questions was also to get some indication from them as to whether charismatic and expository preaching can coexist as a solidified method of preaching God's word.

The interviewees understood both preaching methods but had slight differences concerning charismatic dogma. Pastor Watson reasons that God's word should be the center of their ministry and preaching for all gospel ministers. Believers should not base their spiritual walk on experience as it pertains to the Spirit's gifts but should live by God's word.

However, Pastor Watson does not rule out the Holy Spirit's work but emphasizes God's word. He recognizes that the Holy Spirit's gifts are active in the church but stresses the need to focus on God's Word. Therefore, Pastor Watson disagrees with charismatic dogma because of their focus on spiritual gifts as defining a believer's spiritual walk with Christ. Thus, from his perspective, these preaching methods are separate.

Deacon Ford's view is more along the lines of spiritual experience. He recognizes that it is God's word and the Holy Spirit that empower the church. From his perspective, the Holy Spirit is the source that inspired God's word through human agents, and it is the Holy Spirit that empowers the preacher to preach the gospel and believers to come to repentance. Deacon Ford's overall Christian view is that both are needed in the life of believers and the church. He argues that we need not only God's word but also the Holy Spirit's guidance and empowerment to fulfill Christ's mandate of the Great Commission to go forth and spread the gospel (Matt 28:19–20). Adding to this argument, Scott Pace argues:

> A theology of preaching begins with the humble acknowledgment that preaching is not a human invention but a gracious creation of God and a central part of His revealed will of the church. Because God has ordained preaching as a designated means for accomplishing his work, we can benefit from tracing the theological root of preaching to the spiritual fruit it produces. God himself, in the person of the Holy Spirit, is the divine agent that unifies all of the elements of preaching, from preparation to proclamation. Our understanding of the Spirit's work in preaching is also a crucial theological component for us to consider . . . the same Holy Spirit who inspired Scripture also works in us as the divine agent

CHAPTER 4: RESEARCH DATA ANALYSIS

of interpretation. Jesus identified him as the "Spirit of truth" who guides us into the truth and discloses God's Word to us (John 16:13–15). He teaches us all things (John 14:26) and enables us to understand spiritual and scriptural truth (1 Cor. 2:10–16). As the one who inspired the Scriptures, the Spirit is able to help us interpret them faithfully and accurately.[5]

Deacon Ford's theological argument presents some merits, as it points to both charismatic and expository preaching being able to exist as one sound preaching method. However, both interviewees believe in the divine work of the Holy Spirit in the preaching process. Although Pastor Watson acknowledges that the same Spirit empowers charismatic preaching, he feels that the two cannot function as a solidified preaching method.

Interviews with Pastor Payne and Deacon Dawson (Zion Sister Missionary Baptist Church)

Interview with Pastor Payne

The interview with Pastor James Payne of Zion Sister Missionary Baptist Church was conducted in the same format. He was asked to first give his thoughts on the case study of these two preaching methods before going forward with the interview questions. He conveyed the following:

> The charismatic movement and preaching have been necessary for the teaching and growth of the church. I feel that experience, as held by charismatics, is essential for growth. That spiritual experience that believers may encounter only brings them closer to God and Christ. Therefore, speaking in tongues and experiencing the move of the Holy Spirit in the church and believers' lives is only confirmation of God's presence. We need that experience to let us know that God is still empowering his people.

---

5. Pace, *Preaching by the Book*, 6–7.

CHARISMATIC AND EXPOSITORY PREACHING

Pastor Payne's opening remarks reveal that he is a charismatic preacher who believes in the Holy Spirit's movement in the church and the lives of his flock. Below is Pastor Payne's response to the five interview questions.

Q 1. What are your expectations on Sunday mornings when entering the sanctuary for worship?

Pastor Payne: "I expect to have an encounter with God with the intent of giving whatever burdens we may have to God. When we worship, God inhabits our praises, and then the anointing flows when we begin to sing and give God honor and glory; the Holy Spirit moves throughout the sanctuary."

Q 2. What are your thoughts on the Holy Spirit? Do you look more to the movement of the Holy Spirit to validate your spirituality in living out God's word as conveyed in Scripture?

Pastor Payne: "Yes, I do look to the Holy Spirit for validation in my spiritual walk with the Lord. The Holy Spirit is the third person of the Godhead. The Holy Spirit is our Comforter and Guide; it is by the power of God's Spirit that we can operate in the body of Christ. The Holy Spirit plays a crucial role in the church. How can I preach without the anointing of the Holy Spirit? The Spirit is needed in our lives; without God's Spirit, our walk is in vain."

Q 3. Do you think that the gifts of the Spirit, such as speaking in tongues and signs and wonders such as the laying on of hands for healing, must be manifested in the church during worship services to give credence that God is still actively empowering the church other than by the power of his word?

Pastor Payne: "From my perspective, the Holy Spirit is always present. The Holy Spirit moves within our hearts and dwells with us. However, to answer that question concisely, the Spirit's gifts, such as speaking in tongues or the laying on of hands, do not have to manifest themselves in the church to prove that God is still actively empowering the church. The Holy Spirit validates God's

CHAPTER 4: RESEARCH DATA ANALYSIS

word and is a witness to the word of God. The Holy Spirit is present to lead, guide, and empower the church. However, if God sees a need for this manifestation of the gifts, it is by his divine authority to do so."

Q 4. Do you feel that a believer must speak in tongues as evidence of being filled with the Spirit?

Pastor Payne: "My answer to this question is a simple no, simply because not everyone speaks in tongues. The gifts of the Spirit are available to the church. Speaking in tongues does not confirm being filled with the Spirit; it is your walk with the Lord and how you live that validates that. Some may be faking speaking in tongues, saying things that people do not understand to be untruthful. That is why we must be careful to validate being filled with the Spirit as it pertains to the Spirit's gifts."

Q 5. Do you, as a believer, feel that God's word is sufficient, or is there a need for the miraculous manifestation of the supernatural in the life of the believer to prove being filled with the Spirit?

Pastor Payne: "No, I do not think that there is a need for the miraculous to prove that one is filled with the Spirit. Just you living by God's word is evidence of being filled with his Spirit. However, I look for the move of the Spirit in all avenues of my life and ministry. Ultimately, it is through living out God's word obediently that people will see the Spirit of God in you."

Interview with Deacon Dawson

The interview with Deacon Leroy Dawson of Zion Sister Missionary Baptist Church was informative. His theological views were in concert with his pastor's views (J. Payne) regarding charismatic and expository preaching. Since Zion Sister Missionary Baptist Church is charismatic, the church embraces much charismatic dogma regarding the Spirit's gifts, preaching, and how they worship and engage in that spiritual experience. Below are Deacon Leroy Dawson's responses to the interview questions.

> Q 1. What are your expectations on Sunday mornings when entering the sanctuary for worship?
>
> Deacon Dawson: "I expect to meet the Holy Spirit; that is my first and foremost expectation. To worship God in Spirit and truth in our church service and beyond. I look for the power of God through his Spirit, because it is the Holy Spirit that illuminates God's word in the believer through the man of God that delivers his word every Sunday morning."
>
> Q 2. What are your thoughts on the Holy Spirit? Do you look more to the movement of the Holy Spirit to validate your spirituality in living out God's word as conveyed in Scripture?
>
> Deacon Dawson: "I recognize that the Holy Spirit is the agent that leads and guides the church in all truths about God, Christ, and his word. The Holy Spirit moves believers by touching their hearts regarding righteousness in the Lord. The Holy Spirit convicts the hearts and minds of believers concerning sin and ungodly living. So, I look for the Holy Spirit to validate my spiritual walk. Although I stand firmly on God's word, it is the Holy Spirit that validates that stance, because the Spirit dwells in us."
>
> Q 3. Do you think that the gifts of the Spirit, such as speaking in tongues and signs and wonders such as the laying on of hands for healing, must be manifested in the church during worship services to give credence that God is still actively empowering the church other than by the power of his word?
>
> Deacon Dawson: "No, I do not think the gifts of the Spirit need to manifest themselves in the church to show that God is actively empowering the church. We come together in one place on Sunday for fellowship and worship; the spiritual gifts can be displayed anywhere if God wills it. God cannot be put in a box; this is what caused the Jews to lose sight; they looked more

CHAPTER 4: RESEARCH DATA ANALYSIS

to the presence of the ark of the covenant than to God himself. God can manifest these spiritual gifts through believers at any time."

Q 4. Do you feel that a believer must speak in tongues as evidence of being filled with the Spirit?

Deacon Dawson: "No, I do not think that speaking in tongues is evidence of being filled with the Spirit. Not all Christians speak in tongues; however, we all have gifts. It all depends on God and how he bestows them on the church."

Q 5. Do you, as a believer, feel that God's word is sufficient, or is there a need for the miraculous manifestation of the supernatural in the life of the believer to prove being filled with the Spirit?

Deacon Dawson: "I think that God's word is enough, because every time you open your eyes, it is a supernatural event, but God's word is forever; it is supernatural on its own."

Interview Summary for Pastor Payne and Deacon Dawson

Interviewing these two leaders from Zion Sisters Missionary Baptist Church provided tremendous input into this research. Both the pastor and deacon chairperson leaned more toward the experience of the Holy Spirit. However, they emphasized that we cannot neglect God's word's playing a critical role in believers' lives. Pastor Payne and his deacon chairperson acknowledge the importance of the Holy Spirit in church ministry.

Neither Pastor Payne nor Deacon Dawson dismissed the charismatic dogma and its theology concerning spiritual gifts within the church. Both conveyed that the Holy Spirit enables the preacher to preach God's word with truth and power and is always present to guide the church in the ways of the Lord. They see that both are necessary in fully presenting the gospel to the world and within the church's foundations in fellowship. Although they did provide their theological thoughts on some critical aspects of charismatic teachings, what was not conveyed was their position on how this affects the preaching methods of charismatic and expository preaching. Nonetheless, the information received indicates that they are charismatically indoctrinated—they are not alienating expository preparation as it pertains to the preaching process. For them, preaching is at the core of spreading the gospel.

The interviewees demonstrated a zeal for God's Spirit and his word, which is needed in the preacher's life and in the lives of all believers. Charismatic and expository preachers concur in that the Holy Spirit is active in confirming God's word; without the Spirit, there is no power, because the Holy Spirit validates all truth from the Father and the Son (see John 14:15–21, 15:26, 16:7–15). The preachers are the instrument God uses to convey his word to his people. As Peter Adam states, "God accommodates himself so completely to the theological, emotional, and spiritual needs of his people through his preachers."[6] Therefore, the same God empowers both preaching methods, regardless of what interpretive issues may exist, because it is the Holy Spirit who reveals all truth of God's word.

Analysis of Questionnaire Responses

The next phase of this case study on charismatic and expository preaching involved a questionnaire. Three congregational members from each church completed a ten-question questionnaire; however, their names are only known to me. The members were informed that their participation would be confidential, thus allowing them to be more genuine in answering the basic yes-or-no questions. The complete list of the ten questions is available in

---

6. Adam, *Speaking God's Words*, 142.

CHAPTER 4: RESEARCH DATA ANALYSIS

Appendix B: Research Questionnaire. A total of nine members completed the questionnaire. Below are the results that show the answers of the participants from each church to the questionnaire given, which provides data on how believers view charismatic and expository preaching and on their theological positions on questions about the Holy Spirit and the gifts the Holy Spirit bestows upon the church. A questionnaire completed by some of these church members gives theological insight into how members of the church's congregation perceive these preaching methods/teachings.

Results

Q 1: This question relates to speaking in tongues, which is a charismatic practice. There were nine participants, three from each of the churches, that participated in this case study. All three members from New Hope answered yes to speaking in tongues, the three Mount Olive members responded no, and the three Zion Sister members answered yes. Therefore, 90 percent of the participants believe in speaking in tongues. It is interesting that the three New Hope members believe in speaking in tongues, as they attend an expository-based church.

Q 2: Members of these three churches were asked if they believe that healing is still active in the church, and 89 percent answered yes, with only one answering no.

Q 3: Participants were asked if they believe the Holy Spirit still empowers the church, and 100 percent said yes.

Q 4: This question dealt with the members' perspectives on whether expository preaching is the best preaching method to reach believers and nonbelievers, and 100 percent answered yes, which is surprising, considering that Zion Sisters is a charismatic church.

Q 5: This question was constructed to get insight into how believers perceive charismatic preaching—whether it is a new wave of the Holy Spirit's movement. All participants answered no. Again, the members from Zion Sisters Baptist Church followed the others in answering no, which is intriguing, because they identify as charismatic.

Q 6: Each participant was asked which preaching method they prefer, and 89 percent chose expository preaching versus charismatic. One member from Zion Sisters picked expository.

Q 7: Participants were asked if they speak in tongues, and 44 percent answered yes, while 56 percent answered no.

Q 8: All participants answered no when asked if the spiritual gifts ceased with the apostles, 100 percent agreeing that the spiritual gifts are still active in the church in this modern age.

Q 9: This question asked church members if charismatic preaching appeals to all age groups, and 89 percent said yes.

Q 10: The final question asked if the church members think expository preaching should incorporate some charismatic methods, and 100 percent said yes.

Final Analysis of Case-Study Findings

Researching charismatic and expository preaching methods yielded some interesting findings. It was surprising that most of those who participated in this study did not dismiss what charismatics hold theologically, and and agree that charismatic preaching is moved by the Holy Spirit. However, it was unfortunate that because of the COVID-19 pandemic, only three churches were able to participate. The case study consisted of interviews with the pastors and deacon chairpersons, and three members from each church who completed questionnaires. The churches that participated were New Hope Missionary Baptist Church, Mount Olive Baptist Church, and Zion Sisters Missionary Baptist Church.

The interview data obtained from these pastors and deacon chairpersons reveals a strong stance on the word of God being the ultimate authority in their preaching and deacon ministry.

CHAPTER 4: RESEARCH DATA ANALYSIS

However, both the pastors and the deacon chairpersons of these churches recognized that the Holy Spirit is the agent by which they are empowered. Therefore, both charismatic and expository preaching methods rely on the Holy Spirit in their preaching ministries. Theologically, both preaching methods' interpretations of Scripture concerning the Holy Spirit's work in the church are not that far apart. Although charismatics embrace the Holy Spirit's gifts and the experience of believers as confirmation of being filled with God's Spirit, it does not mean that the Holy Spirit should be negated. As Christians, we all desire to be filled with God's Spirit, to experience that divine power of God that only his Spirit can bestow.

Furthermore, without the Holy Spirit, ministry is in vain. The same Holy Spirit who inspired Scripture is the same Spirit that dwells in us to help interpret Scripture.[7] As Pace asserts, "Jesus identified him as the 'Spirit of Truth' who guides us into the truth and discloses God's Word to us (John 16:13–15)."[8] These interviews substantiated the hypothesis that charismatic and expository preaching are intertwined and that, when combined, they can be a valuable model for preaching in this modern age.

The pastors and deacon chairpersons who participated in this study acknowledged that the spiritual gifts are active in the church; preferably, they are used depending on how the Spirit bestows them to each believer, but the Spirit's gifts are present in the church. All the members who participated in the questionnaire embraced charismatic dogma but were steadfast in asserting that God's word is the ultimate authority Christians should cling to for Christian living. The results of this case study show that Christians embrace expository preaching but also need charismatic flair in the way God's word is presented. Although the participants were steadfast in holding to the authority of God's word, the charismatic approach is not neglected, for every believer should stand on and live according to God's word, for God's word is life-giving. The Holy Spirit's experience and gifts are only there to enhance one's spiritual walk as a child of God and in obedience to Christ.

7. Pace, *Preaching by the Book*, 7.
8. Pace, *Preaching by the Book*, 7.

Conclusion

There have been other studies on this topic, as cited in this research. However, there is much more work to be done on this subject. This case study has shown the fruit of these preaching methods if combined for the church's edification. The same Spirit that empowers the expository preacher does the same for the charismatic. It is the Holy Spirit that leads and empowers the church and all its ministries. We cannot dismiss charismatic doctrine solely because of some errors in interpretation.

Those interpretations can be rectified with sound exegesis, hermeneutical skills, and prayer, asking the Spirit to guide in understanding the Scriptures. The data acquired reveals that charismatic preaching is an anointing from God bestowed by his Spirit, so we can embrace this method and spread the gospel better. Nonetheless, there is tremendous work to be done in preaching from a combination of the charismatic and expository perspectives, which can only bless the church.

Chapter 5: Final Conclusion and Findings

Introduction

Preaching is the ultimate tool in the church's ministry through which the gospel is conveyed in every community. The effectiveness of the charismatic and expository preaching methods is not a new concept to preaching. The ability to preach from a charismatic or expository perspective is evident throughout the Bible. This case study on charismatic and expository preaching has provided insight into preaching methods that have been beneficial to the church's spiritual and numerical growth for many years.

Moses was both charismatic and expository in his approach when speaking to the Israelites in Deut 4–6 concerning obedience, idolatry, God's law (Ten Commandments), and loving the Lord. Even Jesus presented a charismatic and expository flare throughout his three years of ministry before going to the cross. Therefore, this case study's main objective was to identify these two preaching methods and determine if these preaching methods could be integrated as a solidified preaching approach for the local church's spiritual and numerical growth.

Therefore, a series of interviews were conducted, and questionnaires were completed by three church members from each church that participated in this case study. The interviews conducted with the pastors and deacon chairpersons from each church and the questionnaires supported this case study's thesis. The findings revealed that charismatic and expository preaching are intertwined, solely because both methods depend on the Holy Spirit's empowerment. Preachers rely on the Holy Spirit's help in their ministry, because it is the Spirit that reveals all truth of Christ as being the word of God.

Finding 1

In interviewing the three pastors of the churches that participated, all the pastors conveyed that God's word is front and center in their preaching ministry. Although two of the pastors were expository-based preachers, the other was charismatic but unequivocally expository in how he presented God's word. However, all the interviewees expressed that the Holy Spirit is the driving force in their ministry. They all concur in that the gifts of the Spirit are available and active in the church today. However, two out of three of the pastors believe that if the word of God is going forth with power, the manifestation of spiritual gifts is not necessary.

Even with the questionnaires, the findings are the same, as the members leaned more toward God's word being preached with power from the Holy Spirit than looking for the spiritual gifts to be manifested in worship services. The church members, like their pastors, prefer reliance on God's word rather than the outward manifestation of spiritual gifts such as speaking in tongues and the laying on of hands during worship services. However, they acknowledged the crucial role of the Holy Spirit in the church. The members interviewed believe that charismatic and expository preaching are beneficial in the ministry, but they prefer sound doctrine over spiritual showboating.

The deacon chairpersons are more inclined to see the active manifestation of the Holy Spirit in the church service. It is confirmation that what is being said and done in the worship service is of God. The deacon chairpersons insisted that if the Holy Spirit is upon the man of God, he will preach only the truth of God's word, which will come forth and fill the hearts of those present. The deacon chairpersons believe strongly in the manifestation of

CHAPTER 5: FINAL CONCLUSION AND FINDINGS

the gifts of the Spirit. Also, they think both preaching methods are intertwined for the edification of the church.

Finding 2

This case study revealed that believers within the church desire that God's word be preached unadulterated. However, there still is a need for the manifestation of the Holy Spirit in believers' lives. The pastors, deacon chairpersons, and members agreed that God's word is what all Christians live by spiritually. They attested that the Holy Spirit energizes and guides the body of Christ (the church). The results of the interviews and questionnaires succinctly reflect that charismatic and expository preaching is effective in worship services. However, there is a contrast when it comes to numerical growth in the local church.

What could be ascertained from this study is that churches that are charismatic or even trying to balance the two preaching methods experience a more significant numerical increase than expository-based churches. Zion Sisters Baptist Church is charismatic and has a large membership; Mount Olive Baptist Church is expository based but has a balance of the charismatic approach in the worship service and has an adequate membership of roughly eighty.

New Hope Missionary Baptist Church is succinctly expository and has only thirty members, with little or no growth. When attending Mount Olive's and Zion Sisters' church services in the past, I observed robust worship services filled with God's Spirit and excitement. From this observation, one can only ascertain that people gravitate to this type of spiritual energy and that the church grows as a result.

Charismatic preaching with this type of spiritual life excites the people, and if expository preachers exhibit this same spiritual energy, then there is no difference if God's word pierces the hearts of those listening. Since the Holy Spirit is the agent that empowers both charismatic and expository preachers, then everything is in order, as God would have it to be. However, the main issues still reside in the different interpretations of certain scriptures that divide the two approaches. Those differences deal with the Holy Spirit's movement and the gifts he bestows on believers in ministry. This case study failed to ascertain why these hermeneutical issues have divided the two preaching methods, because there are solid arguments for the Spirit's gifts being active and not ceasing with the apostles' deaths. Therefore, further research on this subject could reveal more insight into these issues. Although an abundance of research has been conducted on this subject, as conveyed in the literature review in chapter 1, there is still room for more.

Results Compared to Previous Studies in This Literature Review

Compared to other research studies on charismatic and expository preaching, this study's results are minimal. Further studies are broader than this case study. For instance, Peter Adam's approach is a practical theology of expository preaching; he asserts, "Preaching is addressed to the congregation. The great advantage of this is that it provides an opportunity to address the believers assembled as the Body of Christ. Preaching is essentially a corporate activity, and its most useful aim is corporate edification."[1]

From Peter Adam's perspective, all preaching has one universal goal: corporate edification of the body of Christ. Both charismatic and expository preaching are solidified in this quest for edifying the church with preaching. Then, there is Jerry Vines and Jim Shaddix's work *Power in the Pulpit*, which argues for the power in the pulpit from an expository approach. Their study is based on preparing and delivering a powerful sermon from the pulpit.

Their research is significant, because it is the premise of this case study's hypothesis, which is that charismatic and expository preaching are intertwined and can be integrated as a solidified preaching method. Both charismatics and expository preachers follow the rules of preparation in preparing a sermon. However,

---

1. Adam, *Speaking God's Words*, 70.

CHAPTER 5: FINAL CONCLUSION AND FINDINGS

with charismatics, the difference is the charisma in delivery fueled by the Spirit, although, in contrast, expository preachers can exhibit the same kind of appeal and still be expository based. Vines and Shaddix argue that the call to preach is precisely that—a call to preach.[2] From their perspective, the call to preach is much more than just preaching; it is also a call to prepare.[3] This case study's research explored this aspect of preaching from a charismatic and an expository viewpoint and concluded that this is a path that all preachers must take in their preaching ministry.

Dr. Jerry Vines is an expository-based preacher and a homilist in his own right who believes "we must seek the Spirit's anointing in our preaching."[4] This statement from Dr. Vines is very significant, because the results of this research show that believers stand and live by God's word; however, the Holy Spirit's power must be the guiding force in their lives and ministry, from their perspective. Dr. Vines is very profound in his assertion regarding the Spirit's anointing as it pertains to preaching. He acknowledges the following:

> We must seek the Spirit's anointing. Ask him to come on you and your message. Allow Him to manifest His power in and through you. Never be satisfied with anything less in your sermon delivery. You may not always experience the power of the Holy Spirit upon your preaching in equal measure. For reasons in the realm of the mysterious, there are times when the anointing comes upon us in larger measure than at other times . . . But there should be such a surrender of life to the Spirit that every time we preach, there is evidence of God's blessings upon us.[5]

Charismatics and expository preachers drink from this same well, the waters of the Holy Spirit. Therefore, as much as sermon preparation is crucial, it cannot supplant reliance on the Holy Spirit

---

2. Vines and Shaddix, *Power in the Pulpit*, 13.
3. Vines and Shaddix, *Power in the Pulpit*, 13.
4. Jerry Vines, qtd. in Bill Bennett, "The Secret of Preaching with Power," in Akin et al., *Text-Driven Preaching*, 57.
5. Vines and Shaddix, *Power in the Pulpit*, 13.

to perform the supernatural work that only he can accomplish in lives and ministry.[6] Expository preachers and their congregations would do well to seek that spiritual power and life that charismatics vigorously stand on. Charismatics, in turn, need the solid biblical teaching that is found in expository preparedness. Achieving this would solidify both preaching methods.

This research reveals that charismatic and expository preaching are not as opposed as one may think; the key that both share is their need for the Spirit's power in their ministry. For instance, when asked, "How do you know that the Holy Spirit dwells within you?" The typical answer from a charismatic perspective is as follows: "I know that the Holy Spirit dwells within me because I have experienced it. I have spoken in tongues."[7] However, from an expository perspective, the answer would be the following:

> The biblical answer is found in Romans 8:9, "But ye are not in the flesh but in the Spirit, if so be that the Spirit of God dwells in you. Now, if any man have not the Spirit of Christ, he is none of His." If a person does not have the Holy Spirit, then he is not His. He does not belong to Christ. He is not a Christian. If I am a saved person, then I have the Holy Spirit. How do I know? I know so because God says so. All who believe in Christ have received the Spirit (John 7:39). Paul said, "The Holy Spirit dwelleth in us" (2 Timothy 1:14), and this is true of every blood-bought child of God. According to God's definition (1 Cor. 6:19; John 7:39), a Christian is one who is indwelt by the Holy Spirit and thus has received the Spirit. There is no such thing as a person who is justified by faith but who has not received the Spirit. The fact of the Spirit's reception and indwelling presence is not based on some subjective and questionable experience. It is based upon the direct statements of the Word of God.[8]

The Scriptures are unequivocal in the idea that all who belong to Christ have the Holy Spirit dwelling within them. From

6. Pace, *Preaching by the Book*, 103.
7. Zeller, "Charismatic Movement," 3.
8. Zeller, "Chrismatic Movement," 3.

CHAPTER 5: FINAL CONCLUSION AND FINDINGS

conversion and baptism, the Spirit is with the believer. Scripture conveys to believers that those who belong to Christ have the Holy Spirit to lead and guide them in life and ministry. The Holy Spirit confirms the word of God, by which all Christians live. Charismatics are correct in their assertion that believers should possess the gifts of the Spirit in some measure. However, even if a believer does not display any spiritual gifts, that does not mean that the person has not received the Holy Spirit. The Spirit's gifts are there for the church to spread the gospel, and they have not ceased.

What seems to be the great divide between the two preaching methods is their understanding of the Holy Spirit's function in believers' lives and ministry. To negate this problem, it is incumbent on believers, especially pastors and deacon chairpersons, to understand that both charismatics and expository preachers stand on God's word and yield to the Holy Spirit, who reveals all truth and leads and guides the church. It is God that determines when and where the gifts of the Spirit will be manifested for his glory.

Sound contextual exegesis of Bible passages regarding these matters of the Holy Spirit and the Holy Spirit's gifts to the church is needed.[9] Most importantly, the charismatic assertion that spiritual gifts are still active in the church has merit. According to Paul in 1 Cor 13:8–12, these gifts will cease when Jesus Christ returns. The need for these gifts will end when he comes, and we will be caught up to meet him in the air and will be changed "from mortal to immortal."[10]

For now, the gifts are needed to help spread the gospel and fight the darkness of this fallen world that Satan has a hold on.[11] Arguably, expository preachers have disagreed with this interpretation because they believe that the gifts ceased with the apostles' deaths. If this were the case, it would mean that the Holy Spirit is limited in his work in empowering the church. For these two preaching methods to coexist in harmony for the church's betterment, they must agree to disagree in love. It is the Holy Spirit

9. Hanson, "What is a Charismatic?," para. 15.
10. Hanson, "What is a Charismatic?," para. 15.
11. Hanson, "What is a Charismatic ?," para. 15.

that empowers all preaching from God's pulpits. Beata Urbanek correctly asserts, "According to the teachings of the New Testament, the Spirit always stands behind the words of God spoken by man: 'For no prophecy ever came through human will, but rather human beings moved by the Holy Spirit spoke under the influence of God' (2 Peter 1:21)."[12]

What is implied here is that regardless of the preaching approach, be it charismatic or expository, preachers are called by God and are empowered by the Holy Spirit to preach. So, there is common ground here for both to build upon in ministry that will edify the church and advance the gospel. As Urbanek notes, "The assistance of the Holy Spirit while preaching the word and its presence in the herald of God's message is at the fore in the chronological and logical order. If a man is to preach the word of God, he must have direct contact with Him and thus supernatural access to God's truth."[13]

Therefore, without God's consent and his Spirit, neither preacher—charismatic or expository—has the power of God in his delivery, and the words they speak are of human origin, not of God. Josh P. S. Samuel acknowledges, "There are some Pentecostal preachers (charismatics) who not only mishandle Scripture in their sermons but also rely on hype to generate responses that appear to be supernatural."[14] Samuel notes that these same preachers often claim that the Spirit leads them to do what they do.[15]

If it is of God, it will stand and be fruitful according to God's will. Members of the churches from this case study preferred sound biblical preaching over manifestations of the spiritual gifts in worship services. They realized that sometimes, it could be all for show and not of God, as God's word cannot be faked. In implementing this research, what emerged was that regardless of the preaching approach, "God is actively involved in the process,"

12. Urbanek, "Holy Spirit Acting," 245.
13. Urbanek, "Holy Spirit Acting," 347.
14. Samuel, "Spirit in Pentecostal Preaching," 199.
15. Samuel, "Spirit in Pentecostal Preaching," 199.

CHAPTER 5: FINAL CONCLUSION AND FINDINGS

and both preaching methods can stand together, producing fruit for the kingdom of God.[16] All the research done on this subject still could not dismiss charismatic doctrine and preaching as it is presented today. There are valid arguments from both sides, which has only created an impasse. Nevertheless, God and his Spirit empower all preaching perspectives, both charismatic and expository. As Samuel explains:

> God is more interested in developing messengers than messages, and because the Holy Spirit confronts us primarily through the Bible, we must learn to listen to God before speaking for God. God's role in preaching is critical, as the Spirit must first deal with the preacher and subsequently with the congregation for effective preaching through Scripture.[17]

Charismatic and expository preachers are jewels of the ministry who have blessed the church for many years. All the studies that have been conducted on the issue of these preaching methods have only touched the surface of the theological problems confronting these methods. However, these problems can easily be mitigated by a hermeneutical and exegetical approach. Josh Samuel states, "Spirit baptism is a gift that any Christian can receive by faith within the context of praise and prayer . . . and there is a difference between a preacher who has received Spirit baptism and one who has not.[18] Samuel explains, "Those who have not experienced Spirit baptism are like the disciples on whom Christ breathed and to whom he said, 'Receive the Spirit' before the Day of Pentecost."[19] What is needed for all preachers of the gospel is the spiritual power that only the Holy Spirit can provide.

---

16. Samuel, "Spirit in Pentecostal Preaching," 201.
17. Samuel, "Spirit in Pentecostal Preaching," 203.
18. Samuel, "Spirit in Pentecostal Preaching," 204.
19. Samuel, "Spirit in Pentecostal Preaching," 204.

Final Conclusion

This case study was informative concerning charismatic and expository preaching. Many expository preachers do not realize that they are charismatic because it is the Holy Spirit at work. All participants in this case study recognize that the Holy Spirit confirms the word of God. Based on this case study, I conclude that charismatic and expository preaching can be integrated.

The charismatic approach to preaching has drawn young and old to the church, and those churches that are expository based and balanced by the charismatic flare have also drawn people to Christ and his church. The power of the charismatic movement could not be significant if it were void of the Spirit of God. Therefore, both preaching methods are intertwined because of the Holy Spirit. Believers see the effectiveness of both methods regarding the edification of the church. Thus, I hypothesize that charismatic and expository preaching can be solidified and integrated, even with issues from a biblical perspective that seem to divide both preaching methods.

The issues concerning the work of the Holy Spirit before and after a believer's conversion could be rectified simply by understanding that "because God is love, the Holy Spirit pours God's love into our hearts (Rom 5:5; 15:30; Col 1:8) and often the strongly manifested presence of the Holy Spirit will create an atmosphere of love. Because God is not a God of confusion, but of peace (1 Cor 14:33), the Holy Spirit brings an atmosphere of peace."[20] By love through the power of the Holy Spirit, these preaching methods are solidified.

The Holy Spirit dwells in both charismatic and expository preachers. Only one Spirit is part of the Godhead, and this same Spirit (the Holy Spirit) is what unifies charismatic and expository preaching. Because God is not divided, through the Holy Spirit, there is commonality, which love solidifies. Love, through the Holy Spirit between the two preaching methods, will prevail. The research conducted has shown that charismatic and expository preaching can

---

20. Grudem, *Systematic Theology*, 644.

CHAPTER 5: FINAL CONCLUSION AND FINDINGS

be solidified for the church's edification and can be a tremendous tool in spreading the gospel. Combining these two preaching methods empowered by the Holy Spirit's incredible power will strengthen the church's mandate to witness and spread the gospel.

The future of preaching will revolve around these methods of preaching, simply because solidification of the two approaches will enable preaching with the power of the Spirit to sustain it, but preachers must commit to the proper tasks of hermeneutics, exegesis, and homiletics to guarantee its future.[21] In a world in need of its Creator, God's word must continue to go forth for all to hear. Preaching is the tool that informs sinners and the saved about Christ and God's love; if anyone is going to be saved, they must call upon the name of the Lord. Paul, in Rom 10:13, conveys this to the believers in Rome. However, he also notes, "How can they call on the one they have not believed? And how can they believe in the one of whom they have not heard? And how can they hear without someone preaching to them?" (Rom 10:14). We need preaching.

---

21. Stevenson, *Future of Preaching*, 65.

Appendix A

Research Interview Questions

Name and title: _____

Name of church: _____

Date: _____

The following questions are part of a research case study on charismatic and expository preaching methods pertaining to the body of Christ's edification and growth.

1. What are your expectations on Sunday mornings when entering the sanctuary for worship?

2. What are your thoughts on the Holy Spirit? Do you look more to the movement of the Holy Spirit to validate your spirituality in living out God's word as conveyed in Scripture?

APPENDIX A: RESEARCH INTERVIEW QUESTIONS

3. Do you think that the gifts of the Spirit, such as speaking in tongues and signs and wonders such as the laying on of hands for healing, must be manifested in the church during worship services to give credence that God is still actively empowering the church other than by the power of his word?

4. Do you feel that a believer must speak in tongues as evidence of being filled with the Spirit?

5. Do you, as a believer, feel that God's word is sufficient, or is there a need for the miraculous manifestation of the supernatural in the life of the believer to prove being filled with the Spirit?

Appendix B

Research Questionnaire

Name: _____

Name of church: _____

Date _____

1. Do you believe in speaking in tongues?

    yes or no

2. Do you believe that healing is active in the church?

    yes or no

3. Do you believe the Holy Spirit still empowers believers to do miracles?

    yes or no

4. Is sound expository preaching the best method for reaching the saved and unsaved?

    yes or no

5. Do you believe that charismatic preaching is a new wave of the Spirit?

    yes or no

APPENDIX B: RESEARCH QUESTIONNAIRE

6. Do you prefer charismatic preaching or expository preaching? (circle one)

   charismatic or expository

7. Do you speak in tongues?

   yes or no

8. Do you believe that speaking in tongues and the other spiritual gifts ceased with the apostles?

   yes or no

9. Do you believe charismatic preaching appeals to all age groups?

   yes or no

10. Do you think expository preaching should incorporate some charismatic methods?

    yes or no

Appendix C

Consent Form (Pastor)

The Liberty University Institutional
Review Board has approved this document for use from
6/19/2020 to—
Protocol #4103.061920

CONSENT FORM

Charismatic and Expository Preaching:
A Case Study of Two Preaching Methods within the
Local Church

Lewis D. Mathis
Liberty University
Rawlings School of Divinity

For pastors and deacon chairpersons: You are invited to be in a research study on charismatic and expository preaching. This study seeks to determine if charismatic and expository preaching and methods can be integrated as one sound doctrine for church growth, teaching, and the edification of the body of Christ. You were selected as a possible participant because you are eighteen years of age or older and you are the pastor or deacon chairperson at one of the churches chosen to participate in this study. Please

APPENDIX C: CONSENT FORM (PASTOR)

read this form and ask any questions you may have before agreeing to be in the study.

Lewis D. Mathis, a doctoral candidate for a doctor of ministry in biblical studies at the Rawlings School of Divinity at Liberty University, is conducting this study.

Background information: The purpose of this study is to determine if charismatic and expository preaching can coexist as one sound biblical doctrine for the growth and teaching of the church. From an expository preaching perspective, on the day of Pentecost, the apostle Peter preached the first sermon that established Christ's church. Thousands of people were added by the movement of God from hearing this gospel, which was from the foundation of creation. It was given first to the Jew and then to the gentiles (Acts 2:14–47). This very fact is compared with the charismatic movement and preaching methods this research is to explore. The questions to be answered regarding this research are as follows: (1) Is the charismatic movement in this modern age a new movement of the Holy Spirit? (2) Should Christians embrace this movement and its practices and teachings as the vehicle for church growth? From a theological perspective, Peter's first sermon was charismatic, grounded in expository preaching with the powerful movement of the Holy Spirit (Acts 2). Therefore, this research has the fundamentals of sound biblical doctrine as its theological basis to determine if, in fact, these two approaches/methods of preaching (charismatic and expository) can be integrated into sound biblical preaching and teaching as one fundamental doctrine for church growth in the local church.

Procedure: If you agree to be in this study, I will ask you to do the following:

1. After the Sunday worship service, I will meet with the pastor and chairperson for an interview session.

APPENDIX C: CONSENT FORM (PASTOR)

2. The pastor and deacon chairperson will be asked some interview questions concerning charismatic and expository preaching. The interviews will be conducted as one-on-one sessions, with the approximate time being thirty minutes for each participant.

3. I will observe the worship service in order to compare charismatic and expository preaching methods within the church.

Risks: The risks involved in this study are minimal, which means they are no more than what you would experience in everyday life.

The Liberty University Institutional
Review Board has approved this document for use from
6/19/2020 to—
Protocol #4103.061920

Benefits: Participants should not expect to receive a direct benefit from taking part in this study. However, this research may provide the church with a concise understanding of two preaching methods that will help the church grow and understand the word of God from a charismatic and an expository perspective.

Compensation: Participants will not be compensated for participating in this study.

Confidentiality: The data of this study will be kept private. Research data will be stored securely, and only I will have access to this data. I will assign pseudonyms to participants. Data will be stored on a password-locked computer; however, the code list will be secured in my locked file cabinet for the next three years upon completing the study. Then, all data will be disposed of by shredding the materials.

Voluntary nature of the study: Participation in this study is voluntary. Your decision of whether or not to participate will not affect your current or future relations with Liberty University or your church. If you decide to participate, you are free not to answer any questions or withdraw at any time without affecting those relationships.

APPENDIX C: CONSENT FORM (PASTOR)

How to withdraw from the study: If you choose to withdraw from the study, please contact me. Should you decide to withdraw, data collected from you will be destroyed immediately and not included in this study.

Contacts and questions: If you have any questions or concerns regarding this study and would like to talk to someone other than me, **you are encouraged** to contact the Institutional Review Board at 1971 University Blvd., Green Hall Ste. 2845, Lynchburg, VA, 24515, or by email at irb@liberty.edu.

Please notify me if you would like a copy of this information for your records.

Statement of consent: I have read and understood the above information. I have asked questions and have received answers. I consent to participate in the study.

_____
Signature of participant   Date

_____
Name of church

_____
Signature of investigator   Date

Appendix D

Consent Form (Church Member)

The Liberty University Institutional
Review Board has approved this document for use from
6/19/2020 to—
Protocol #4103.061920

CONSENT FORM

Charismatic and Expository Preaching: A Case Study
of Two Preaching Methods within the Local Church
Lewis D. Mathis
Liberty University
Rawlings School of Divinity

For church members: You are invited to be in a research study on charismatic and expository preaching. This study seeks to determine if charismatic and expository preaching and methods can be integrated as one sound doctrine for church growth, teaching, and the edification of the body of Christ. You were selected as a possible participant because you are eighteen years of age or older and a church member at one of the churches chosen to participate in this study. Please read this form and ask any questions you may have before agreeing to be in the study.

APPENDIX D: CONSENT FORM (CHURCH MEMBER)

Lewis D. Mathis, a doctoral candidate for a doctor of ministry in biblical studies at the Rawlings School of Divinity at Liberty University, is conducting this study.

Background information: The purpose of this study is to determine if charismatic and expository preaching can coexist as one sound biblical doctrine for the growth and teaching of the church. From an expository preaching perspective, on the day of Pentecost, the apostle Peter preached the first sermon that established Christ's church. Thousands of people were added by the movement of God from hearing this gospel, which was from the foundation of creation. It was given first to the Jew and then to the gentiles (Acts 2:14–47). This very fact is compared with the charismatic movement and preaching methods this research is to explore. The questions to be answered regarding this research are as follows: (1) Is the charismatic movement in this modern age a new movement of the Holy Spirit? (2) Should Christians embrace this movement and its practices and teachings as the vehicle for church growth? From a theological perspective, Peter's first sermon was charismatic, grounded in expository preaching with the powerful movement of the Holy Spirit (Acts 2). Therefore, this research has the fundamentals of sound biblical doctrine as its theological basis to determine if, in fact, these two approaches/methods of preaching (charismatic and expository) can be integrated into sound biblical preaching and teaching as one fundamental doctrine for church growth in the local church.

Procedure: If you agree to be in this study, I will ask you to do the following:

1. Complete an anonymous questionnaire, which should only take about thirty minutes or less.

Risks: The risks involved in this study are minimal, which means they are no more than what you would experience in everyday life.

APPENDIX D: CONSENT FORM (CHURCH MEMBER)

Benefits: Participants should not expect to receive a direct benefit from taking part in this study. However, this research may provide the church with a concise understanding of two preaching methods that will help the church grow and understand the word of God from a charismatic and an expository perspective.

Compensation: Participants will not be compensated for participating in this study.

The Liberty University Institutional
Review Board has approved this document for use from
6/19/2020 to—
Protocol #4103.061920

Confidentiality: The data of this study will be kept private. Research data will be stored securely, and only I will have access to this data. Data will be stored on a password-locked computer for the next three years upon completing the study. Then, all data will be disposed of by shredding the materials.

Voluntary nature of the study: Participation in this study is voluntary. Your decision whether or not to participate will not affect your current or future relations with Liberty University or your church. If you decide to participate, you are free not to answer any question or withdraw at any time without affecting those relationships.

How to withdraw from the study: If you choose to withdraw from the study, do not complete and return your questionnaire, and please contact your pastor, so the pastor can choose someone else to participate.

Contacts and questions: If you have any questions or concerns regarding this study and would like to talk to someone other than me, **you are encouraged** to contact the Institutional Review Board at 1971 University Blvd., Green Hall Ste. 2845, Lynchburg, VA, 24515, or by email at irb@liberty.edu.

September 2, 2020

Dear brothers and sisters in Christ:

As a graduate student at the Rawlings School of Divinity at Liberty University, I am conducting research as part of the requirements for a doctorate in ministry. The purpose of the study is to determine if charismatic and expository preaching can be integrated as one sound doctrine that edifies the body of Christ as a movement of the Spirit of God. Therefore, I am writing to invite congregants to participate in this study.

If you are eighteen years of age or older, a member of the church congregation, and would like to participate, you will be asked to complete a questionnaire. The questionnaires will be anonymous, as no identifying information will be collected. It should take approximately thirty minutes to complete.

If you are a pastor or deacon chairperson and would like to participate, you will be asked to answer some interview questions that will last approximately thirty minutes per participant. I will also observe the entirety of the worship service and note the order of the worship service, music selection, speakers' method of approach, speakers' sermon text, exposition of the text, and the congregation's response. Your name and other identifying information will be requested as part of your participation, but the information will remain confidential.

To participate, please let your pastor know that you are interested. If you are a member and are selected to participate, you will be given the questionnaire at the end of the worship service.

APPENDIX D: CONSENT FORM (CHURCH MEMBER)

Since the questionnaires will be anonymous, congregants will not need to sign a consent form; but if you are a pastor or deacon chairperson, a consent form will need to be signed in advance of the interview, and you will return the form at the time of the interview. The consent form will contain additional information about the research.

Sincerely,

Lewis D. Mathis
Candidate for Doctor of Ministry Degree

IRB APPROVAL

LIBERTY UNIVERSITY.
INSTITUTIONAL REVIEW BOARD

June 19, 2020

Lewis D, Mathis

IRB Exemption 4103.061920: Charismatic and Expository Preaching: A Case Study of Two Preaching Methods within the Local Church

Dear Lewis D. Mathis,

The Liberty University Institutional Review Board has reviewed your application in accordance with the Office for Human Research Protections (OHRP) and Food and Drug Administration (FDA) regulations and finds your study to be exempt from further IRB review. This means you may begin your research with the data, safeguarding methods mentioned in your approved application, and no further IRB oversight is required.

Your study falls under exemption category 46.101(b)(2), which identifies specific situations in which human participants research is exempt from the policy set forth in 45 CFR 46:101(b):

APPENDIX D: IRB APPROVAL

(2) Research that only includes interactions involving educational tests (cognitive, diagnostic, aptitude, achievement), survey procedures, interview procedures, or observation of public behavior (including visual or auditory recording) if at least one of the following criteria is met:

> (i) The information obtained is recorded by the investigator in such a manner that the identity of the human subjects cannot readily be ascertained, directly or through identifiers linked to the subjects;

> (iii) The information obtained is recorded by the investigator in such a manner that the identity of the human subjects can readily be ascertained, directly or through identifiers linked to the subjects, and an IRB conducts a limited IRB review to make the determination required by §46.111(a)(7).

Please note that this exemption only applies to your current research application, and any changes to your protocol must be reported to the Liberty IRB for verification of continued exemption status. You may report these changes by submitting a change in protocol form or a new application to the IRB and referencing the above IRB Exemption number.

If you have any questions about this exemption or need assistance in determining whether possible changes to your protocol would change your exemption status, please email us at irb@liberty.edu. Sincerely,

G. Michele Baker, MA, CIP

Administrative Chair of Institutional Research

Research Ethics Office

Liberty University | Training Champions for Christ since 1971

VITA

Dr. Lewis D. Mathis

PERSONAL

    Born: March 7, 1967

    Married: Phyllis D. Mathis, July 4, 1996

    Children: Tekela Mathis, Danielle Mathis, Dominique Mabry, and nine grandchildren

EDUCATIONAL

    BS, Liberty University, 2015

    MDiv, Liberty University, 2017

MINISTERIAL

    Licensed: May 2005

    Ordained: February 2020

PROFESSIONAL

    Chairperson of Trustee Board

    Associate Pastor of New Hope Missionary Baptist Church

PROFESSIONAL SOCIETIES

    Alpha Lambda Delta Honor Society

Bibliography

Adam, Peter. *Speaking God's Words: A Practical Theology of Expository Preaching.* Downers Grove, IL: InterVarsity, 1996.

Akin, Daniel L., et al., eds. *Text-Driven Preaching: God's Word at the Heart of Every Sermon.* Nashville, TN: B. & H. Academic, 2010.

Berkley, James D. *Leadership Handbook of Preaching and Worship: Practical Insight from a Cross-Section of Ministry Leaders.* Grand Rapids: Baker, 1997.

Carson, D. A. *Showing the Spirit: A Theological Exposition of 1 Corinthians 12–14.* Grand Rapids: Baker, 2019.

Culpepper, Robert H. *Evaluating the Charismatic Movement: A Theological and Biblical Appraisal.* Valley Forge, PA: Judson, 1977.

Elwell, Walter A. *Evangelical Dictionary of Theology.* 2nd ed. Grand Rapids: Baker Academic, 2001.

Fee, Gordon D. *The First Epistle to the Corinthians.* Grand Rapids: Eerdmans, 2014.

———. *God's Empowering Presence: The Holy Spirit in the Letters of Paul.* Grand Rapids: Baker Academic, 1994.

Forbes, James. *The Holy Spirit & Preaching.* Nashville: Abingdon, 1989.

Gaffin, Richard B., Jr. *Perspectives on Pentecost: New Testament Teaching on the Gifts of the Holy Spirit.* Grands Rapids P. & R., 1979.

Grudem, Wayne A. *Systematic Theology: An Introduction to Biblical Doctrine.* Grand Rapids: Zondervan, 2000.

Hand, Chris. "The Legacy of the Charismatic Movement." http://media.sermonaudio.com/articles/cr-11309133345-1.PDF.

Hanson, Eric. "What is a Charismatic?" February 7, 2008. https://www.sermoncentral.com/sermons/what-is-a-charismatic-eric-hanson-sermon-on-holy-spirit-in-believers-118311.

Heisler, Greg. *Spirit-Led Preaching: The Holy Spirit's Role in Sermon Preparation and Delivery.* Nashville: B. & H. Academic, 2007.

Klein, William W., et al. *Introduction to Biblical Interpretation.* Nashville: Thomas Nelson, 1993.

Lea, Thomas D., and David Alan Black. *The New Testament: Its Background and Message.* Nashville: B. & H., 2003.

BIBLIOGRAPHY

MacArthur, John F., Jr. *Ashamed of the Gospel: When the Church Becomes like the World.* Wheaton, IL: Crossway, 2010.

———. *The Charismatics.* Grand Rapids: Zondervan, 1979.

———. *Charismatic Chaos.* Grand Rapids: Zondervan, 1992.

McComas, Kenny. *Childish Carnal Cantankerous Charismatic Corinthians: An Analytical Study of the Tongues Movement.* Rittman, OH: Wm. K. McComas, 1978.

McDonnell, Kilian. *Charismatic Renewal and the Churches.* New York: Seabury, 1976.

Meyer, F. B. *Expository Preaching: Plans and Methods.* Eugene, OR: Wipf & Stock, 2001.

Mohler, R. Albert, Jr. "The Charismatic Movement: Cause for Celebration or Concern?" *SBC Life*, January 1, 2000. https://www.baptistpress.com/resource-library/sbc-life-articles/the-charismatic-movement-cause-for-celebration-or-concern/.

Nathan, Rich, and Ken Wilson. *Empowered Evangelicals: Bringing Together the Best of the Evangelical and Charismatic Worlds.* Boise, ID: Ampelon, 2009.

Olford, Stephen F., and David L. Olford. *Anointed Expository Preaching.* Nashville: B. & H., 1998.

Orrick, Jim Scott, et al. *Encountering God through Expository Preaching: Connecting God's People to God's Presence through God's Word.* Nashville: B. & H. Academic, 2017.

Pace, R. Scott. *Preaching by the Book: Developing and Delivering Text-Driven Sermons.* Nashville: B. & H. Academic, 2018.

Poloma, Margaret M. *The Charismatic Movement: Is There a New Pentecost?* Boston: Twayne, 2014.

Ray, Jeff D. *Expository Preaching.* Grand Rapids: Zondervan, 1940.

Samuel, Josh P. S. "The Spirit in Pentecostal Preaching: A Constructive Dialogue with Haddon W. Robinson's and Charles T. Crabtree's Theology of Preaching." *Pneuma* 35.2 (2013) 199–219. https://doi.org/10.1163/15700747-12341314.

Schmit, Clayton J. "Key Principles of Preaching." *Voice*, Spring 2011. https://fullerstudio.fuller.edu/key-principles-of-preaching.

Sensing, Tim. *Qualitative Research: A Multi-Methods Approach to Projects for Doctor of Ministry Theses*, Eugene, Oregon: Wipf & Stock, 2011.

Stevenson, Geoffrey. *The Future of Preaching.* London: SCM, 2010.

Stitzinger, James F. "The History of Expository Preaching." *Masters Seminary Journal* 3.1 (Spring 1992) 5–32. https://tms.edu/wp-content/uploads/2021/09/tmsj3a.pdf.

Suurmond, Jean-Jacques. *Word and Spirit at Play: Towards a Charismatic Theology.* Grand Rapids, MI: Eerdmans, 1995.

Taylor, Mark. *1 Corinthians: An Exegetical and Theological Exposition of Holy Scripture.* The New American Commentary 28, edited by E. Ray Clendenen. Nashville: B. & H., 2014.

BIBLIOGRAPHY

Thomas, Derek W. H. *Acts*. Reformed Expository Commentary. Phillipsburg, NJ: P. & R., 2011.

Towns, Elmer L. *The Gospel of John: Believe and Live*. Twenty-First Century Biblical Commentary Series 4. Chattanooga, TN: AMG, 2002.

———. *A Journey through the New Testament: The Story of Christ and How He Developed the Church*. Mason, Ohio: Cengage Learning, 2008.

———. *Theology for Today*. Mason, Ohio: Cengage Learning, 2008.

Unger, Merrill F. "Expository Preaching." *Bibliotheca Sacra* 111.444 (1954) 324-37.

Urbanek, Beata. "The Holy Spirit Acting in the Message of the Word of God." *Ruch Biblijny i Liturgiczny* 71.1 (2018) 341-61. https://rebus.us.edu.pl/bitstream/20.500.12128/18028/1/Urbanek_The_Holy_Spirit.pdf.

Vang, Preben. *1 Corinthians*. Teach the Text Commentary Series. Grand Rapids: Baker, 2014.

Vines, Jerry, and Jim Shaddix. *Power in the Pulpit: How to Prepare and Deliver Expository Sermons*. Chicago: Moody, 1999.

Vondey, Wolfgang. *The Holy Spirit and the Christian Life: Historical, Interdisciplinary, and Renewal Perspectives*. New York: Palgrave Macmillan, 2014.

White, Douglas M. *He Expounded: A Guide to Expository Preaching*. Chicago: Moody Press, 1952.

Whitesell, Faris D. *Power in Expository Preaching*. Westwood, NJ: Fleming H. Revell, 1963.

Zeller, George W. "The Charismatic Movement: 35 Doctrinal Issues." https://www.middletownbiblechurch.org/doctrine/charis35.pdf.

www.ingramcontent.com/pod-product-compliance
Lightning Source LLC
Chambersburg PA
CBHW070912160426
43193CB00011B/1437